The Exam Skills Handbook

Palgrave Study Skills

Pocket Study Skills
Series Editor: Kate Williams

The Exam Skills Handbook

Achieving Peak Performance

2nd edition

Stella Cottrell

palgrave
macmillan

First edition 2007
Second edition 2012

Published by
PALGRAVE MACMILLAN

Palgrave Macmillan in the UK is an imprint of Macmillan Publishers Limited, registered in England, company number 785998, of 4 Crinan Street, London N1 9XW.

Palgrave Macmillan in the US is a division of St Martin's Press LLC, 175 Fifth Avenue, New York, NY 10010.

Palgrave Macmillan is the global academic imprint of the above companies and has companies and representatives throughout the world.

Palgrave® and Macmillan® are registered trademarks in the United States, the United Kingdom, Europe and other countries

ISBN 978-0-230-35854-6

This book is printed on paper suitable for recycling and made from fully managed and sustained forest sources. Logging, pulping and manufacturing processes are expected to conform to the environmental regulations of the country of origin.

A catalogue record for this book is available from the British Library.

A catalog record for this book is available from the Library of Congress.

Printed and bound in China

Contents

Acknowledgements

In writing this book, I am grateful to all those students and former students who talked so openly to me about their exam experiences. In particular, I thank those who were prepared to take risks experimenting with new strategies when their former strategies didn't seem to be working, and those who were willing to share their ideas about exams and what worked for them over the years.

I would like to thank staff at Palgrave for the energy and expertise they bring to drawing the book together, especially Suzannah Burywood and her team for orchestrating the publication of the book, and Rachael Hardy and her team for ensuring it reaches the bookshops. I offer my grateful thanks to Caroline Richards for editing the script and preparing it for the printers.

Finally, I thank those who sustained me through the writing process, feeding and watering me, hoovering and dusting, proofreading and checking information, and taking me for walks. I hope I can offer such support in return.

S.C.

Chapter 1

Introduction

This book takes a completely different approach to exams. It looks at them through the filter of extra-ordinary experience, which can lead to exceptional personal performance.

Most advice on exams treats them as, at best, a necessary evil that you can manage for better or worse. That makes sense to a certain extent as, in the lead-up to exams, it can feel as if we are entering into a scary cavern of the unknown.

By contrast, this book takes as its starting point the view that you can take charge of your preparation in a manner similar to that used by sports champions. They approach the most challenging events in ways that help them attain an optimum mental state for gaining their personal best. High performers refer to this as the 'zone'. You can approach your exams with such a mind-set.

Taking charge of the process

There are things we can do to increase the likelihood of a better exam experience for ourselves. This means not just better marks in exams, but greater clarity and control over the exam process:

- more understanding of what exams are for,
- more understanding of our own performance,
- awareness of better coping strategies,
- awareness of what we can do to achieve greater success.

Achieving personal best

If you adopt even basic, common-sense strategies for exam preparation, the chances of passing your exams are very high. This book provides guidance on how to maximise such chances of success.

However, athletes are rarely content simply to complete a race; they seek continually to improve on their personal best, taking a broad approach to all aspects of their training.

They work towards entering a zone where they feel calm, focused and confident of achieving their personal best.

Similarly, this book encourages you to take holistic, systematic and strategic approaches to exam preparation, which can help you achieve the best possible results, or your 'peak performance'. You may enter a 'zone' similar to that of athletes, where taking an exam feels easy and even enjoyable.

How to use this book

This book aims to assist you to:

- feel positive about taking exams,
- reflect upon what exam success means to you personally,
- build your confidence in taking exams,
- plan more effectively for your exams,
- develop useful revision and exam strategies and techniques,
- take a broad-based approach to exam preparation,
- cope with emergencies,
- achieve your personal best.

Different starting places

The book is designed so you can start at different places depending on:

- what you need,
- how much time you have to revise,
- how good at exams you are already,
- what you want to achieve, at what cost.

New to exams?

You don't have to start at the beginning of the book or work through it chapter by chapter. However, if you are very anxious about exams, or have not been successful in them recently, then this Introduction and Chapter 2, 'Where do I start?' will orientate your thinking about exams. Chapters 7 and 9 outline basic revision strategies.

Confused about exams?

Clarify your thinking with Chapters 5 and 6 on exam myths and what examiners are looking for.

Anxious and stressed about exams?

To identify suitable ways of managing your anxiety, see Chapter 10.

Wasting time in revision sessions?

Make better use of revision time by using the structured revision sessions in Chapter 9.

Worried about memory?

Train your memory through techniques outlined in Chapter 8, but see Chapter 10 on the impact of stress management, mental calm, relaxation and nourishment. Structured revision (Chapter 9) is also relevant.

Want to achieve peak performance in exams?

Even if you are already good at exams, you may wish to do better. See Chapters 3, 4 and 11, on getting into the 'exam zone'.

Lots of time before the exam?

Look at sections on building knowledge architectures (Chapter 8), and on paced revision through structured sessions (Chapter 9).

Does exam ace work? (*continued*)

Most of us have been given advice about what to do or not to do in order to be better students and pass our exams:

Don't leave all your revision until the last minute

Last-minute revision always works best for me

Beware advice. Experiment to find out what really works for you.

It is important that we practise and experiment with different strategies so that we know from experience what is really effective for us in particular circumstances and for different kinds of learning. We can then feel confident in accepting or declining advice.

Individuals perform well under very different conditions.

Students' differing experiences

I do work hard all through the year, but I do my most effective revision the week or so before the exam – that's when all the connections start to fall into place.

My housemates revise through the night sometimes, and they seem to do OK. I don't know how they do that – it doesn't work for me, I need my sleep so for me it is essential to start preparing well in advance of the exam.

I know everyone says don't stay up revising the night before an exam, but that's the best way for me to remember dates and names.

I read somewhere that memorising material was a superficial approach to study and that students who do this are not very successful. I find this hard to believe because I have always memorised things like lists of information and I have always had very good exam results.

Once I am in the exam, I won't remember things if I haven't been over it and over it. This means I can't just start revising the week before the exam. I have to build up my sense of the subject by looking at it from different angles over many weeks.

It really depends for me what kind of thing I am trying to remember. I need to keep at the work on a regular basis to get to grips with it. That way, I know I know 'the big stuff', like the people and what their contributions were. Even if I do that, I still end up working like mad for the last few days, going over the fine details.

I learnt some of my best little gems by reading my notes in the corridor on the way down to the exam room, and outside the exam room door. I know this goes against all advice in the books, but details that seemed trivial when I was trying to revise concepts suddenly struck me as useful examples when I was about to go into the exam.

Reflection

What lessons could you learn from these students' experiences?

What affects exam success?

Exam performance is the result of a combination of many factors, not a single cause. Even though we may realise this, when we excel or do badly we tend to revert to simplistic reasons, such as whether we 'got the right questions' or 'not being very good at exams'. If exam success has seemed elusive or inexplicable, then it is worth considering the following contributory factors, and reflecting on how far these are significant to your own situation.

Factors that affect exam performance

1   Subject knowledge
2   Your exam history
3   Exam preparation
4   Exam practice
5   Experience of the subject
6   Writing skills
7   Use of time
8   Attitude and approach

These aspects are covered briefly in the following pages, and most are covered in detail throughout the book.

Reflection

Before you go further, take a moment to consider the 8 factors listed above. Which of these factors do you think have been amongst your strengths in previous exams?

Which factors are likely to be areas that let you down?

What, in general, do you think made your exam marks lower than they needed to be?

1   Subject knowledge

Knowing your subject well

The better you know your subject, the easier it is to:

- recognise what is significant – and to understand what must be included and what you can leave out when revising and when writing exam answers;
- identify links and connections between different aspects of the subject;
- recognise which schools of thought are relevant to which exam questions.

Background reading

You are expected to read a wide range of books and articles to deepen your understanding of the subject. Your reading will be evident in aspects such as the examples and details that you refer to in your exam answers, the way you link material, the judgements you make, and the quality of your analysis.

Subject knowledge is often regarded as the most important aspect of exam success but it is unlikely to be the sole factor. Even if you know a great deal, other factors apart from subject knowledge can be more critical in the exam.

2 Your exam history

The number of exams you sit builds your familiarity with working under exam conditions. Combined with a taste of success, this can help you to approach exams without excessive stress.

A history of exam failure can undermine exam confidence, but does not mean that you can't be good at exams in the future. You *can* improve exam technique.

On the other hand, students who are usually good at exams can become complacent or even bored, which can lose them the competitive edge unless they adopt new approaches.

Reflection My exam history

Consider whether your exam history has left you feeling:

☐ Confident about exams?

☐ With a taste of success?

☐ With a good understanding of how to improve?

☐ With sufficient experience that you can enter exams without excessive nerves?

☐ Ready and keen to find ways of improving your marks?

Overall, how does your exam history affect the way you approach exams now?

3   Exam preparation

The amount of exam preparation

If you want to be really sure of doing well in exams, then it is essential to prepare well for them. It is extremely unlikely that you can go into an exam and do well without such preparation, even if you work hard throughout the course. This is because the exam isn't simply about studying or even understanding the material, but is about presenting:

- specific aspects of what you know, that is, only what the questions ask for;
- in particular ways, such as short answers or essays or demonstrations;
- at speed – there is little time to think, plan and select during an exam;
- from memory: there isn't usually the time or the opportunity to look up anything you can't remember.

In preparing for an exam, there isn't a set amount that you must do. It is more a question of putting aside time, on a regular basis, to focus on the subject in an active and strategic way. As the exam approaches, you need to spend much more time in exam preparation.

The type of preparation

Preparation is about more than learning the material. It includes such factors as:

- creating the right state of mind;
- knowing your weak points and working on them;
- finding support;
- taking care of yourself so that you are physically able to perform;
- organising your life so that you can cope with the lead-up to the exam.

Reflection — Exam preparation

Consider whether your preparation is:

- Too rushed? Do you need to start earlier?
- Too brief? Do you need to do more?
- Boring? Do you need to make it more varied and interesting?
- Lonely or isolating? Would you work better with others?

---

4   Exam practice

One of the best ways of preparing for any event is to practise in conditions as near to the real event as possible. Although it is hard to simulate exam conditions exactly, it is still valuable to go through the process. If you are not used to exams, or suffer from exam nerves, then it is all the more important to work under simulated exam conditions before your exams.

Through exam practice, you:

- gain a sense of how much you can write in a short time; this will help you revise more efficiently, recognising the importance of selecting the most essential material;
- learn to work quickly in planning, writing and checking answers;
- improve at becoming focused quickly;
- discover what you really know and what you only half-remember;
- can check your answers after the event – and see the quality of your answers.

Take and make opportunities

If you are lucky, your programme may set mock exams. If you get the chance of these, do take it. It may not be an enjoyable experience, but you will find out valuable lessons about your own performance before you sit the exam for real. Otherwise, consider setting up your own mock conditions, either alone or with others (see Chapter 9).

Reflection   Exam practice

What would you gain from exam practice?

What stops you from doing exam practice? How can you overcome this?

What do you need to know about your own exam answers that you could find out from practice exams?

Could you set up mock exams with others? What do you need to do to set this up?

5   Experience of the subject

Students who are familiar with their current subject area benefit from:

- an existing good knowledge base in the subject, on which to build;
- awareness of specialist terminology in the subject.

If you are new to the subject, or recently returned to study, it can sometimes take longer to build an underlying sense of the subject. This may mean that many aspects of study take you longer initially; it takes more time to build your expertise.

Speed in reading and comprehension

You may need to read course material slowly while you build your subject comprehension. This may feel frustrating or demotivating, as it can be a slow process looking up words you don't know, and making sense of material with unfamiliar language and concepts. However, be reassured, over time, the initial disadvantage will reduce or disappear.

Knowledge architecture

You will benefit from actively building your knowledge architecture of the subject, so that you can see how new material fits together (see p. 136, Chapter 8). This will help you use time effectively in preparing for exams, as you will have a better sense of what to learn and what to leave out.

Reflection　　Subject experience

Consider whether your study history has left you feeling:

- ☐ Familiar with the specialist vocabulary in the subject?

- ☐ With a good knowledge of your current subject?

- ☐ Able to read quickly in the subject?

- ☐ Able to identify the most significant aspects of the subject, quickly, when reading and writing?

Are there gaps in your study history that are undermining your confidence now as a student?

---

6   Writing skills

For all written exams, exam success is affected by:

- **style:** using a clear, easy-to-read; writing style;
- **vocabulary:** having the vocabulary to express yourself quickly, succinctly and accurately;
- **composition:** using well-structured, reasoned argument;
- **technical writing skills:** using grammar, punctuation and spelling accurately in order to express your case more clearly, and to ensure the examiner remains focused on the quality of your argument, and not on writing errors.

Students who write well do have an advantage. They can use their language skills to demonstrate their knowledge well, and can sometimes even disguise what they don't know. It is worth developing your writing skills.

Poor writing skills?

If your writing skills are not yet strong, there are things you can do.

- Look for courses where you can develop academic skills, such as critical thinking, writing clearly and structuring an argument. These skills are essential for most university programmes and improve the quality of your writing.
- If you have poor grammar, spelling or punctuation, check whether your university or a local college offers sessions to improve these.
- Take extra care in checking through your exam answers.

If you have always had poor technical writing skills despite working on these, it may be worth checking whether you are dyslexic (see p. 257).

Reflection 📖 Writing skills
Consider whether your exam results might be affected by your writing skills. Which aspects of your writing need most attention?
What can you do now to improve your writing skills?

7   Use of time

Amount of time

Exam performance is affected by the amount of time you spend on:

- reading around the subject to build up your subject expertise;
- thinking about the subject;
- getting to grips with difficult material;
- how many topics you cover in depth for the exams;
- exam preparation;
- developing techniques to aid recall;
- practising exam questions.

It can be a great advantage simply to have more time available for study and revision. This enables you to do justice to the subject, as well as spending time on relaxation, managing stress, physical exercise and nutrition, all of which also contribute to your ability to do well in exams. It is rare for any student to feel they have enough time to give their subject the attention it deserves.

Time well spent

The way you manage the time available to you can be more important than the overall amount of time. If there are many demands on your time, then the strategies outlined in this book should help you make more effective use of the time available.

Reflection 📖 Use of time

How could you create more time for study and revision?

How could you spend more time on your health, nutrition, stress management and fitness, all of which affect exam performance?

Consider how you can use the time you spend on revision and exam preparation more effectively.

8   Attitude and approach

Our mental preparation for exams is perhaps the most important aspect of all. Our cognitive activity, such as our ability to think clearly and logically, is affected by factors such as:

- how calm we are feeling;
- whether we have a sufficient level of interest and excitement;
- the chemicals in the blood stream released by how calm, excited or stressed we are feeling;
- the chemicals we have in the blood stream because of what we consume as food, drink, medication or drugs, or take in from our surroundings;
- how distracted we are by emotions and feelings, rather than being focused on the task in hand.

Our performance is further affected by our attitude in areas such as:

- our motivation and endurance: how well we can keep going when there are other things we would rather do instead;
- our self-understanding: knowing what is likely to be a barrier to good preparation and the steps we need to take to overcome these.

These aspects are addressed in more detail in subsequent chapters.

Reflection 📖 **Attitude and approach**

Does your attitude or level of commitment help or hinder your revision and exam performance?

In which areas of life could you take better care of yourself, so as to improve your exam performance?

What barriers stand in the way of you developing your performance? How can you address these?

Closing comments

Summary ⭐ Key points

★ You can create the conditions for your own success.

★ Aim to look for, and remain focused on, the positives.

★ Take charge of the process.

★ Test and adapt advice to fit your own circumstances.

★ Identify what are the factors that impact most on your current levels of success.

★ Consider how you can use your insights into those factors in order to improve future performance.

★ Adopt attitudes and approaches that will bring success.

This book assumes that people can do well at exams if they understand their subject, practise and prepare well. However, it is important to recognise that the path to exam success isn't the same for everyone. This means that it isn't simply a question of imitating the actions of people who have been good at exams, or following advice that seems to work for some people under certain circumstances.

Part of your exam preparation is testing out what works for you. You need to know whether printed advice or received wisdom works for you. You can develop this knowledge through a number of means, including:

● reflecting on what has happened to you in the past: did it work?
● considering doing things differently if you are not happy with your previous marks;
● testing out a variety of techniques;
● practising, using past exam papers and mock exams.

From this starting point, you can begin to develop sets of practices and states of mind that provide the best possible exam experiences for you.

Chapter 2

Where do I start?

Learning outcomes

This chapter supports you in:
- identifying where to start in your exam preparation
- understanding exams, why they are set and their potential benefits
- developing self-awareness about 'exam success'
- identifying programme expectations
- identifying resources you need for exam preparation
- recognising the most appropriate environment for you to work in

This chapter is designed primarily for those who are new to exams, or who wish to improve their performance but are not sure where to start.

It builds on the introductory chapter in helping you to orientate your thinking about exams. You should be able to work quite quickly through this chapter, as you start your exam preparation.

One way to start is by gaining a solid understanding of what exams are for: if you are going to have to do them, then why are they set, what can you gain from them, and how important is exam success to you?

You can also benefit from thinking through some specific factors that will help settle you into revision, such as:

- the expectations of your programme,
- the best conditions for you to revise,
- the basic tools for exam preparation.

The chart on the following page can help direct you to the most appropriate pages or chapters for your immediate concerns.

Where to start?

Look through the checklist below, and identify the aspects of exam preparation that are most relevant to you now. Tick up to five items that you consider to be priorities for you, and start with these, then come back to this page and identify the next three items. If you are not sure where to begin, browse through the book quickly and see which items catch your eye, and start there.

	Aspect	Pages	Priorities
1	Understanding why exams are set	p. 19	
2	Identifying something positive about exams	pp. 19–21	
3	Deciding what exam success means to you	p. 22	
4	Distinguishing exam myths from reality	Ch. 5	
5	Understanding what examiners want	Chs 6, 13, 14	
6	Knowing where people tend to go wrong with revision and exams	Ch. 7	
7	Finding out how other students approach exams	p. 12	
8	Finding out what is meant by revision	Ch. 7	
9	Knowing what to do in revision sessions	Ch. 9	
10	Understanding what is meant by the 'exam zone'	Ch. 3	
11	Getting in the 'exam zone'	Chs 3, 4, 11	
12	Using revision time effectively to do exam practice	Ch. 9	
13	Taking care of yourself in preparing for exams	pp. 117, 169, 200	
14	Knowing how to succeed in different types of exam	Chs 13, 14	

Why are exams set?

The purpose of exams

Exams are not set merely to make life difficult. They serve various purposes:

- They provide one means of measuring how much you have learnt.
- They enable your tutors to be sure the work they are marking is your own work, not copied from friends, books or the internet.
- They serve as a focus for your study, encouraging you to draw together what you have learnt.

Exams aren't perfect

Exams are not a perfect measure of knowledge and understanding. Some of the areas you know best may not appear on the exam paper, and you may be unlucky to some extent in the questions that are set.

Objective measure

However, exams are designed to be, as far as possible, a fair, objective and impartial way of measuring how far people have learnt what was required as part of the programme.

Coming to terms with exams

You may not like doing exams: most of us could think of things we would rather do. Spending time thinking negative thoughts about exams, such as that they are unhelpful or difficult, doesn't help achieve better marks. Indeed, it is important to come to terms with the reality of exams:

- They count towards your final marks, so it pays to learn how to pass them and to pass them well.
- They do require intense preparation, so you need to take them seriously.
- A reasonable amount of preparation and good exam strategies make it very likely that you will pass.
- Although there are no guarantees with exams, your own preparation is likely to make a difference in how well you perform.
- If you have to do exams, you may as well take a constructive approach to them.

Exams can bring a sense of satisfaction and reward. They provide a reason for putting time aside to really come to terms with a subject, which we might not do if the pressure of the exam were not there. In other words, exams can drive us to perform better, to become experts in a subject.

10 positive aspects of exams

1 Exams can energise us, providing motivation to learn things we would otherwise keep putting off until tomorrow.

2 They provide the incentive to make us look back over what we have already covered in order to check that we really understand it. They encourage us to find ways of remembering information without having to look it up.

3 They can show us what we really know, as opposed to what we thought we knew. We are likely to discover aspects we need to know better, and even to learn more than we realised we could.

4 They require us to manage our time and to plan well; this can help us to develop better project management skills.

5 They provide us with a challenge. If we learn to cope with them, we are likely to emerge stronger, more able to cope with other challenges in our lives, irrespective of the marks we get in the exam. With enough practice and revision, most people can get through exams, but it takes courage to take the exam in the first place.

6 They offer a chance to gain certificates that are passports to further progress.

7 We realise more keenly all the things we would rather do than exams – so that we appreciate these all the more.

8 Exams are usually objective: you can do well in them even if you don't get on well with your tutor.

9 They provide an opportunity to catch up and succeed even if you haven't worked hard all year.

10 You are more likely to feel a sense of expertise if you prepare well for an exam.

Reflection

Which of these positive aspects of exams matters the most to you?

Benefits of exams to me

To build your motivation, take some time to identify the benefits of exams to yourself.

Circle the items that apply to you.

I prefer exams to coursework

Facing a challenge

Providing an incentive to master the material

Objective marking

Conquering fear of exams

The examiner won't know it is my paper s/he is marking

Developing skills in working at speed

Revising with other people

Developing time-management skills

I'll have a sense of achievement

© Stella Cottrell (2006, 2012) *The Exam Skills Handbook*, Palgrave Macmillan

What other benefits are there to exams from your own perspective?

How can you use these advantages to keep you motivated?

What does 'exam success' mean for me?

Exam success can mean different things to different people. Whilst exams are important as part of your programme, it is also essential to keep exams in perspective. Exams are only of relative importance: there are always other things which are more important, such as your life, your mental well-being, your health, family and friends.

Exam success usually comes with some cost. Preparation takes a great deal of time. It uses mental energy, and the stress can have an impact upon ourselves and others.

Each individual has to decide the balance of the 'cost' in relation to the 'gain'. For example, for one person, doing nothing but exam preparation for three months is the cost they are willing to pay in order to revise in the way they feel suits them best.

Another person may feel that less time spent on revision is worth the risk of lower marks, if this reduces the impact of their exam preparation on the people around them or provides a better work–life balance.

Identify programme and exam expectations

As early as possible in your programme, and before you start revising, identify what it is that you are supposed to know. This knowledge should serve as a starting point for investigating your chosen subject, but shouldn't restrict your interest into other areas.

About your programme

The programme outline
Most university and college programmes now provide an overview of what students are expected to know.

Programme objectives
These provide a broad overview of the purpose of the programme.

Learning outcomes
These describe several broad areas of learning that you should have acquired by the end of the programme.

Skills you are meant to acquire
These may be practical skills required within the subject areas, and transferable skills that you should be able to apply within other subject areas or life more generally. These are not necessarily examined.

Syllabus
The syllabus usually describes in greater detail what you are expected to know about different aspects of the programme. You should use this to identify which topics you need to cover as part of your exam preparation.

Handbooks and regulations

You are normally provided with information and guidance about the programme in a Programme, Course, or Student Handbook. These usually contain information about the subject, assessment methods and assessment criteria. Exam Regulations are usually long, detailed and technical. You are likely to be sent a copy of these or given a website to check them. It is your responsibility to check the information: don't expect tutors to tell you what you need to do or know.

Past papers

Past papers provide one of the most valuable ways of gaining a sense of what is expected from you. If the questions seem unfamiliar, it is worth checking whether the syllabus was different when the previous exam was set. These papers are usually available on university websites or in the libraries. For external exams, you can normally request exam papers from the Awarding Body.

Tools for exam preparation

Large pieces of paper or lining paper to chart ideas

Water for hydration

evidence for … .

Mobile device for recording and listening to course material

Index cards or postcards to summarise key points

Some new material to stimulate ideas

Time

Good sleep

Coloured marker pens to highlight different kinds of information

Other students to revise with

Decide on your environment (1)

1 Underline the characteristics below that provide a *desirable* environment for your exam preparation.
2 Then circle the characteristics you consider to be *essential* to the environment for your exam preparation.

sociable

quiet places

well away from university

where I can play music

without distractions

where there is water

where I can pick at food

where there is lots of space for me to draw big colourful diagrams of the course material

on campus

where there are journals and books to stimulate my interest

where I can talk about my ideas out loud

while travelling

in creative chaos

in an organised space

at home

where I can walk about

where I won't be disturbed

away from home

where I can't have my mobile on

the same place each time

a good view

outdoors

different places to give me variety

with computer access

inside

Decide on your environment (2)

For each aspect of exam preparation, identify the kind of environment that you require; consider which location you will use in each case.

Aspect of exam preparation	Location/characteristics of the environment needed to study
To draw up a revision timetable	
To complete your notes	
To reduce notes to more manageable amounts	
To practise writing exam answers	
To go over material to develop your understanding of difficult topics	
To memorise names, dates, facts and figures	
To organise information to assist memory in the exam	
To revise material with other students	
To test your recall of the material	
To do last-minute revision	

Students' experiences

One year, I found out where my favourite bands were playing and I travelled round to the different venues. I spent all day revising on trains and coaches and in cafés, and rewarded myself with a concert each night. I didn't get caught up in everyone else's worry about exams, and I knew I had something to look forward to at the end of every day. It wasn't just a good way for me to revise – it was one of my best experiences ever. It was fantastic.

I never know where to start – which means I often don't get started until it is far too late.

I spend all my time planning and very little actually revising – something I need to get in better balance.

The only way I can revise is when everyone else has gone to bed. This is good for reworking all my notes without being interrupted, but I'm always half asleep in my seminars, and then having to catch up on those at night too.

I was dreading revision – I didn't know what it was and I certainly didn't want to do it. I dragged myself to the library to stop myself getting distracted – and then it was brilliant. No interruptions. All the space I needed. No one asking me to do things for them. Suddenly, I had the peace and quiet to actually take things in. I started to understand it. I felt elated. Without exams, I probably would never have had this experience.

Revision: I went to the shopping centre and sat in the restaurant area with cappucinos, cake and my notes hour after hour. The perfect excuse to escape the house and kids.

I did try to do what you are supposed to do, eating healthily and I drank loads of water. But I just had to eat enormous amounts of sweets and chocolates before I could get down to work. We all did actually, and our marks didn't seem to suffer. Maybe, we had a need for instant energy for all that thinking!

Closing comments

Summary Key points

★ Exams mean different things to different people.

★ Decide what level of 'success' you want.

★ Make exams your own.

★ Identify the personal benefits of taking exams.

★ Invest time and energy that match your goals.

★ Find out as much as you can about the exam.

★ Consider what kind of study environment you prefer.

★ Identify what kind of study environment helps you achieve.

★ Create an environment for exam preparation that is right for you.

This chapter offers some structured activities to help orientate your thinking about exam preparation, and to get you started on planning your revision activity. It provides a series of tools to help shape your early thinking and planning. If you have used the tools and activities provided, then you should have developed a sense of:

● what exams are for;
● what you want to get from exams;
● ways you can think more positively about exams;
● materials and tools you need to support the revision process;
● the right working environment for your exam preparation;
● the initial planning that is required;
● what you can look forward to after the exam.

Such initial setting of the scene can be useful in orientating your thinking towards exam preparation and in making sure you have what you need when you need it. Preparing your mind for revision is just as important as preparing your environment and notes.

Chapter 3

Getting in 'the zone' (i): Planning for peak performance

Learning outcomes

This chapter supports you in:

● understanding the concept of 'peak performance'
● considering the experience of 'the zone'
● identifying your own response to 'critical moments' that affect peak performance
● evaluating your personal characteristics for managing peak performance
● formulating a plan to help you achieve your best performance

Students who do extremely well at exams tend to create a state of mind, or 'mental space', that promotes excellent performance. This mental space helps them persevere with revision, and to approach exams in ways that maximise their chances of success.

Leading athletes and other sports people often employ coaches or psychologists to help them achieve a mental state that promotes peak performance. Achieving this can generate a particular experience referred to as 'the zone'. A similar experience is possible for other activities that require high levels of challenge and personal input, including mastery of a subject for exams.

You can develop self-awareness, build motivation, sharpen your focus, and find the drive needed for achieving peak performance. This can mean performing at levels you hadn't thought possible for you.

Most people have a good common-sense understanding of the things they could do to achieve peak performance. High achievers, however, tend to be better at following through on that common sense, using a systematic approach. The reflections, activities, plans and checklists in this book provide a structure for enabling you, too, to plan systematically towards achieving peak performance.

Peak performance

What is 'peak performance'?

'Peak performance' refers to your own best possible, or 'optimal' performance. This is the performance that you could achieve if everything that is within your control to manage is managed as it should be. It is a potentially motivating concept – something to work towards. How much it motivates rather than restricts us depends very much on our attitude and the common sense that we apply.

The challenge of the absolute 'peak'

Peak performance is a challenge. Your best possible performance is the maximum you would be able to achieve, so it assumes the highest possible levels of input from you. That would mean:

● the maximum hours you could revise;
● the most effective use of all that time;
● using every legal method to achieve your best mental powers;
● optimal strategies for revising and taking exams;
● thorough understanding of your own ways of achieving, including areas you need to improve and the strategies that work for you.

The realistic 'peak'

In reality, it is highly unlikely that 'the maximum' is attainable in every aspect of your preparation and performance. It is natural to have times when things don't go to plan. There will be times when we have to attend to unexpected business, or are unwell, or something we need is not available. You may not *want* to achieve your absolute best in exams – there may be other things that matter more to you. Pages 59–60 look at the importance of realistic goals as a part of attaining peak exam performance. It is for you to decide what would be your ideal outcome for the particular set of exams.

Diminishing returns

Peak performance obviously requires effort as well as strategy. However, part of the planning for peak performance is about ensuring you don't arrive at a point of 'diminishing returns'. This point is very common in the revision process and is recognisable: you feel you are working longer to achieve less. When this happens, students make different responses:

● 'you might as well stop as there is no point';
● 'you might as well battle on, as you need to, even though it seems pointless';
● 'you need to take a break and/or take a different approach'.

Peak performance (*continued*)

It may seem obvious that a short break, some activity, a light snack or drink or a change of scene will refresh you, making it more likely that you can continue with a particular revision session. Similarly, time off from academic study in the week can bring you back to study with more energy and interest. However, this common-sense approach can be difficult to put into practice.

The pressure of exams can make it difficult for students to give themselves permission to stop for a while. It is important to recognise the point of diminishing returns, and to act constructively in maximising your use of time, rather than simply working for longer and longer hours.

Broad-based approach

You can also plan well to avoid entering the point of 'diminishing returns'. This means finding the balance between revision and other activities that enable you to revise effectively.

If you were an athlete, for example, you would look at all those aspects of your life that contribute to your achieving your best on the day of the competition. You wouldn't expect an athlete to turn up for a race looking exhausted, depressed, their stomach rumbling because they haven't time to eat, gasping for a drink of water, lacking the appropriate kit. If their coach asked why they were in such a condition, it wouldn't be acceptable to argue that they put all their time into practising their running and so didn't have time to take care of everything else.

Increasingly, athletes, business people and others are recognising that it is not effective to take a single-minded approach to the most obvious aspects of a task. Other features, such as building psychological motivation, ensuring good health, and attaining a 'work–life balance', are more likely to yield the best results.

What is 'the zone'?

Being 'in flow'

'The zone' is a state of mind and of being, where you experience everything working exactly as it should be in order to achieve your end goal. Csikszentmihalyi (1992) refers to this state as being 'in flow', as everything appears to flow well.

In this state, there is a feeling of enjoyment. You feel good, and confident that you will achieve your personal best. You have heightened awareness of what you are doing, your thinking is positive, and your mind is sharply focused on how you will succeed.

Athletes and 'the zone'

Jackson and Csikszentmihalyi (1999) described athletes' experiences of being 'in flow' once they were completely absorbed in an activity. Athletes can experience this as:

1 **Challenge–skills balance:** finding the correct balance between their current level of skill and the challenges they take on.
2 **Transcending normal awareness:** feeling they are in a very different state of experience, with a heightened state of awareness.
3 **Knowing where they're going:** having a clear sense of purpose and being able to envisage success and the route to it.
4 **Focusing on the present:** doing what they need to do in the longer term by being clear how the current moment contributes to that end goal, and then just doing what needs to be done.
5 **Controlling the controllables:** being aware of what lies within their power to influence, and doing so, and not worrying about the things that lie beyond their power.
6 **Focusing on the fun:** finding the enjoyment in what they are doing.

Is 'the zone' just for athletes?

Most research on 'the zone' has focused on sports. However, research by the BBC suggests that video gamers also experience an increased level of 'alpha brain activity' (BBC News, 2002). Alpha activity is associated with complete rest or meditation. This suggests that being 'at one' with an activity, through total absorption in it, can enable a state of mental clarity and focus. Some students also refer to zone-like states of mind as part of their experience of exams.

Reflection 📖 Being in the zone
Have you ever experienced a zone-like state of total absorption, mental clarity and flow? If so, what actions or circumstances helped to create that mental state?

What is 'the exam zone'?

People who are good at exams can also find a way of getting into a state of mind that helps them achieve their best performance, 'the exam zone'. When you are in the exam zone, you feel:

- that everything is coming together in the way you planned and that the exam will work out fine;
- that you understand the subject as a whole;
- that you know how discrete topics fit into the bigger picture: the jigsaw is complete;
- that you can select quickly the most salient points about each topic;
- that you are comfortable about not knowing some material and details as these are unlikely to matter in an exam context;
- that information is organised in your mind in such a way that you will be able to recover it easily when you need it, such as during an exam;
- a feeling of expertise, and pleasure in that feeling of expertise;
- that it is easy to find out more information, as it reinforces, or can be absorbed easily into, what you already know;
- strongly motivated to know more about the subject;
- strongly motivated to ensure your success through taking care of aspects such as rest, creative diversions, nutrition and time management before the exam and in the exam;

- creative in your thinking about the subject; you see new ways of perceiving the material;
- energised by your growing sense that you know what you are doing and can do well.

Reflection

How close do you feel to being in 'the exam zone' at this point?

Do you feel you usually deliver your own best possible performance in exams?

Students' experiences

When I'm ready for exams, I know it. It's like I have a bird's eye view of the subject – in my mind's eye, I am flying over the subject, looking down onto a landscape that has become small, where every detail
I have learnt fits into its place and I can see it all at once.

Sometimes, when I have been preparing for exams for several weeks, I get a feeling that I know the subject as if from the inside. It's like I know it in my insides, and inside out, like there is nothing that I couldn't know about it if I wanted to – it would just click.

When you are in the 'exam zone', you feel excited by the subject, and want to know more. You don't see problems, just things you need to sort out to prove you can do it.

When I start working for a new exam, I absolutely hate it, because I know how much I am going to have to put into it, how much of my life I am going to dedicate to getting the best marks possible, to being at the top of my form. I know I want to write the best exam papers of everyone, to make the examiner sit up surprised, even if I never find out how good they were. But, the upside of all my work is that I reach a point when everything changes, and I move from sort of 'learning' to 'knowing'. I love that moment when I realise that I just understand the subject in my bones and I know how to work it in the exam. I know how it breaks down, what fits into different types of questions. I even want the questions to be difficult so I get a chance to flex my mental muscle.

It's like being mentally fit – and emotionally geared up, ready to take on the exam and any question they throw at me. No, it's more than that: I actually want the chance to try and do better than any one else in the year, maybe better than anyone else has ever done! I want the feeling that I can excel.

Reflection

What can you learn about the 'exam zone' from these students' experiences?

'The zone' at critical moments

Athletes who achieve 'the zone' experience much higher levels of self-esteem and confidence, and are able to block out negative thoughts. When negative thoughts intrude, it is much harder to remain focused at key moments of a competition (Carlstedt, 2004).

It is believed that the ability to stop the transfer of intrusive thoughts from the right brain to the left brain at critical moments is key to achieving peak personal performance. Athletes who are prone to thinking negatively find it much more difficult to achieve 'the zone'.

Self-awareness and 'the zone'

Getting into 'the zone' doesn't happen by accident. It is a frame of mind, or an experience, that arises out of intense practice and reflection upon performance. Jokela and Hanin (1999) suggest that athletes who perform best can also recall and anticipate accurately their levels of pre-competition anxiety. This puts them into a better position for managing their anxiety.

Reflection

1 Have you ever found that self-doubt or anxiety distracted you just at the critical moment?

2 Do you tend to think of self-doubt and anxiety as something you control? Do they control what you achieve?

3 What do you do to manage your anxiety at critical moments, such as just before an exam?

4 Do you feel you are skilled at blocking out negative thoughts so that you can remain focused on your end goals? If not, is this something you could improve?

How do you enter 'the zone'?

'The zone' is rather elusive. People can describe what happens when they feel they are in 'the zone', but, as with other heightened states that are achieved without drugs, it is much harder to say what exactly takes you into it. However, we can identify those characteristics typically associated with being in the zone, and act in ways that make it more likely to achieve the frames of mind associated with peak performance. These characteristics include:

(a) Self-awareness

(b) Repeated practice

(c) Strong desire to beat past performance

(d) Absorption in the task

(e) Staying focused in the present

(f) Knowing where you are going

(g) Controlling anxiety at critical moments

(h) Controlling the controllables

(i) Finding the enjoyment

Characteristics of peak performance

Read through the following characteristics associated with peak performance and consider how far each is true of you. Identify those aspects that you need to work on further.

(a) Self-awareness

1 ☐ I consider self-awareness to be important.

2 ☐ I make a conscious effort to become more self-aware.

3 ☐ I take active steps to monitor my performance.

4 ☐ I take active steps to monitor my attitude.

5 ☐ I know what I do right with respect to revision.

6 ☐ I know what I do right with respect to exams.

7 ☐ I know where I go wrong in revision.

8 ☐ I know where I go wrong in exams.

9 ☐ I know what I need to do to remain strongly motivated.

10 ☐ I know how to keep myself interested in revision activity.

To become more self-aware, I need to . . .

Characteristics of peak performance (1)

(b) Repeated practice

1 ☐ I spend a great deal of time revising.
2 ☐ I spend a lot of time analysing past exam papers.
3 ☐ I spend a lot of time planning exam answers.
4 ☐ I spend a lot of time answering exam questions.
5 ☐ I spend time on areas I find difficult (e.g. introductions, conclusions).
6 ☐ I practise in conditions similar to those of the exam.

To improve in this area, I need to . . .

(c) Strong desire to beat past performance

1 ☐ I set myself goals to gain higher marks than last time.
2 ☐ I identify particular ways of achieving better marks.
3 ☐ I know the areas where I need to improve.
4 ☐ I give myself practice in areas I need to improve.
5 ☐ I plan how I will achieve better marks.
6 ☐ I create the conditions that make improvement likely.

To improve in this area, I need to . . .

Characteristics of peak performance (2)

(d) Absorption in the task

1 ☐ I can remain focused on what I must do.

2 ☐ I can carry through my plans from start to finish.

3 ☐ I don't notice the time passing when I am revising.

4 ☐ I plan my time so it is easy for me to stay focused.

5 ☐ I plan revision activities in such a way that it is easy to stay focused.

6 ☐ I can create a point of interest to every aspect of revision.

To improve in this area, I need to . . .

(e) Staying focused in the present

1 ☐ I can focus on the tasks I need to do well now in order to succeed, rather than thinking only about my final goals.

2 ☐ I avoid wasting time in worrying.

3 ☐ I think clearly and precisely about what I need to do at the time.

4 ☐ I am good at avoiding distractions.

5 ☐ I aim to excel at every aspect of each task I undertake, as I perform it.

To improve in this area, I need to . . .

Characteristics of peak performance (3)

(f) Knowing where you are going

1 ☐ I am clear about what I want to achieve.

2 ☐ I have set my sights on exam goals which it is reasonable to consider achievable.

3 ☐ I know what I need to do to achieve these.

4 ☐ I have a plan that I follow in order to achieve my goals.

5 ☐ I set realistic steps for achieving my goals.

To improve in this area, I need to . . .

(g) Controlling anxiety at critical moments

1 ☐ I am aware of what level of stress produces my best performance.

2 ☐ I know what triggers my anxiety.

3 ☐ I am able to manage my stress levels.

4 ☐ I can remain positive even at critical moments.

5 ☐ I can refocus quickly if I start to feel anxious.

To improve in this area, I need to . . .

Characteristics of peak performance (4)

(h) Controlling the controllables

1. ☐ I avoid dwelling on those areas that lie outside of my control.
2. ☐ I give thought to which areas of success do lie within my control. These are:

[blank box]

3. ☐ I take charge of those areas that are within my control. I achieve this by (doing):

[blank box]

To improve in this area, I need to . . .

[blank box]

(i) Finding the enjoyment

1. ☐ I can find something to interest me in each aspect of my study.
2. ☐ If I am bored, I find a way to make my study more interesting.
3. ☐ I can find genuine enjoyment in most aspects of my subjects.
4. ☐ I set myself challenges and milestones that are motivating and add interest to each revision session.

To improve in this area, I need to . . .

[blank box]

Moving forward

These pages have encouraged you to reflect upon aspects of your approach to exams, or indeed to any goal, that are likely to lead to success. The following pages provide an outline 5-point plan that can help you to achieve peak performance.

5-point plan for peak performance

The following 5-point plan identifies actions you can take to work towards getting in 'the zone' for peak exam performance. No matter how well you do at exams now, this plan is likely to improve your performance.

Point	Action	See
1 **Want it!**	● Take charge of your attitude ● Develop your self-awareness ● Maintain a balanced perspective ● Find the interest and enjoyment	● Chapter 4 ● All chapters ● pp. 56–7 ● pp. 108–10; p. 185
2 **Live it!**	● Rest, nourishment, water and exercise ● Create the environment ● Gain support from others ● Make the time ● Manage stress	● Chapters 7 and 12 ● Chapter 2 ● Chapter 7 ● Chapter 7 ● Chapter 10
3 **Know it!**	● Understand exams and what examiners look for ● Understand your subject inside out: know it in your bones! ● Select what you really need ● Apply your material to specific questions ● Identify which memory strategies work for you	● Chapters 2, 5, 6, 12–14 ● Chapter 8, pp. 135–9 ● Chapters 9 and 12 ● Chapters 9 and 12 ● Chapters 8 and 9
4 **See it!**	● Clarify what exam success means for you ● Walk your mind through the process ● Envisage your success	● p. 22 ● Chapter 11 ● Chapter 11
5 **Do it!**	● Apply revision strategies ● Learn the material in an active way ● Practise answering exam questions ● Use revision time effectively ● Use exam time effectively	● Chapters 7 and 10 ● Chapters 7 and 9 ● Chapter 9 ● Chapters 7, 8 and 9 ● Chapters 9 and 12–14

Getting in the exam zone: Interpreting the plan

Point	Action	For me this means:
1 **Want it!**	● Take charge of your attitude ● Develop your self-awareness ● Maintain a balanced perspective ● Find the interest and enjoyment	
2 **Live it!**	● Rest, nourishment, water and exercise ● Create the environment ● Gain support from others ● Make the time ● Manage stress	
3 **Know it!**	● Understand exams and what examiners look for ● Understand your subject inside out: know it in your bones! ● Select what you really need ● Apply your material to specific questions ● Identify which memory strategies work for you	

Getting in the exam zone: Interpreting the plan (*continued*)

Point	Action	For me this means:
4 **See it!**	● Clarify what exam success means for you ● Walk your mind through the process ● Envisage your success	
5 **Do it!**	● Apply revision strategies ● Learn the material in an active way ● Practise answering exam questions ● Use revision time effectively ● Use exam time effectively	

Implementing the plan

The 5-point plan is flexible – there are no absolutes. What goes into each aspect depends on where your current expertise lies, what you are willing and able to put into the plan, and whether planning in this way suits your style of working. If you have worked through the Introduction and Chapter 1, you may already be implementing part of the plan.

Personal plan

Appendix 4 provides a personal action plan for you to complete the details in line with your own needs, resources and style of working.

Closing comments

Summary ☆ Key points

★ 'Peak performance' is your best or optimal level of performance.

★ Athletes refer to this as 'getting in the zone'.

★ In 'the zone', everything seems to 'flow' easily.

★ You can be in 'the zone' for exams.

★ Systematic approaches support high performance.

★ Self-awareness supports peak performance.

★ Self-evaluation helps develop self-awareness.

★ You can use your self-evaluation to create your own 5-point plan.

The hallmark of the mind-set that leads to peak performance is the ability to conjure up positive attitudes to revision or exams on those days when you really want to be elsewhere doing something very different. Nobody finds that easy. However, it helps if you can develop a personal plan that keeps you focused on your purpose. If you anticipate difficult times and plan a strategy to keep yourself motivated, then it is easier not only to apply yourself to your goals, but also to reduce the 'bad days'.

Apart from good planning, the other key aspect to developing the right mind-set is having an excellent level of self-awareness. The more you know yourself – the triggers that motivate you, and the triggers to negative attitudes – then the better you are able to create the environment and conditions that will maintain and improve a positive frame of mind. These themes are covered further in the next chapter.

Chapter 4

Getting in 'the zone' (ii): Frames of mind for peak performance

Learning outcomes

This chapter supports you in:

- understanding the importance of attitude to exam performance
- developing self-awareness about your attitude to exams
- identifying triggers that are likely to promote or inhibit the right frame of mind
- keeping exams in perspective
- setting realistic goals

This chapter focuses on the first aspect of the 5-point plan: 'Want it!' It looks at ways of creating the best frame of mind for exam success.

It can be easier to study on 'good days' when we feel we will do well in our exams. However, the real challenge is being able to find a spark of positivity on a 'bad day' and to be able to fan this into a feeling of interest and enthusiasm for a task you would rather avoid.

This is something that high achievers tend to be good at. They also tend to have strong self-belief and determination, even if they don't vocalise it to others. Self-belief, in this respect, isn't the same

as brash but empty self-promotion or boasting. On the contrary, it is grounded in high levels of self-awareness developed through thoughtful reflection and experience, and focused on identifying ways of improving performance.

Attitude is the key to successful performance. However, 'attitude' can feel like a rather slippery substance, difficult to get hold of when we need most to be in charge of it. It may seem that it controls us, rather than the other way round.

This chapter provides structured ways of thinking about your attitude, so that you can take charge of it, and use it to achieve your exam goals.

Take charge of your attitude

Why does attitude matter?

We saw above how success for athletes was related to a state of mind. Attitude is, similarly, a key ingredient of success in other areas of life, including exams. Van Overwalle (1989), for example, interviewed students at the start of their course and after their exams. Those with the highest academic self-esteem, expectations of success and effective study strategies achieved the best exam marks.

Students often refer to 'attitude' as if it were a given part of their personality, something they cannot change. However, it is essential to take charge of attitude. You have more control over your exam performance if you:

● keep track of your attitude to revision and exams;
● are able to notice changes in mood that make you feel anxious or otherwise negative about revision and exams;
● are aware of triggers that can affect your attitude, mood or motivation;
● investigate the methods that work for you in improving your attitude to revision and exams;
● are prepared to take action to change your attitude, mood or feelings when you recognise characteristics such as doubt, anxiety or frustration.

Want it!

Point 1 on the 5-point plan is 'Want it!' This means wanting success sufficiently to work for it, plan for it, and put other things aside in order to get what you want, working on your mind and lifestyle as well as with the subject material.

If you wish to be more successful at exams, you need to decide how important this really is for you. Those who do really well at exams generally have a very strong desire to succeed, and invest their time and energy in order to gain the best possible outcome. They tend to be very clear about the significance of the outcome to their short- and long-term goals, and are able to use this to remain focused on action that leads to their success.

Wanting it!

You need to:

● know why the exam is important to you (see p. 22, 'What does "exam success" mean to me?');
● believe it matters;
● devise ways to keep your purpose clearly in mind whilst focusing on interim goals.

How do exams affect me?

Rate how each of the following aspects affects you on a scale of 0–5, where 5 is the highest level of positivity, and 0 is the lowest.

	Aspect	Positivity score					
1	Fear of exams	No fear.. Terrified					
		5	4	3	2	1	0
2	Dislike of exams	Enjoy exams............................ Hate exams					
		5	4	3	2	1	0
3	Motivation to do well on the course	Highly motivated to do well ...... Don't care					
		5	4	3	2	1	0
4	Value given to the qualification	Very high value .... Don't value at all					
		5	4	3	2	1	0
5	Recognition of the benefits of taking exams	Appreciate strongly........ Don't see benefits					
		5	4	3	2	1	0
6	Finding enjoyment in preparation for exams	Enjoy a lot.................No enjoyment at all					
		5	4	3	2	1	0
7	Valuing the learning that comes from preparing for exams	Value highly.................... Don't value at all					
		5	4	3	2	1	0
8	Determination to do well in the next set of exams	Very determined ... Very little determination					
		5	4	3	2	1	0
9	I can become engaged in revision, finding interest in it	Very much so .... Not at all true					
		5	4	3	2	1	0
10	I am energised by a wish to do better in each set of exams	Very energised............. Not at all energised					
		5	4	3	2	1	0
	Total score						

How do exams affect me? Interpreting your score

Scores between 40 and 50

This score suggests that you take an extremely positive approach to your exams, which is a real asset. If your score is accurate, you have strong reserves to carry you through even difficult times.

Scores between 30 and 40

This score suggests a high degree of positive thinking: this should help you with revision and exams. You are well placed to consider those areas where your scores are lower. How could you apply your positive thinking to further improve your attitude?

Scores between 20 and 30

This score suggests an average level of positive thinking. It is likely to benefit you on good days, but you may find it harder to persevere when you need to study but feel bored, demotivated, tired or distracted. It is worth spending time considering ways of raising your levels of commitment and motivation.

Scores between 10 and 20

This score suggests a relatively low level of positive thinking. Your current attitude may make it harder for you to settle down to study and/or to maintain your attention when revising. However, you can take action to change your approach. Start by going through the following pages. Select one or two areas from the table on p. 47 as starting places for thinking more deeply about your attitude.

Scores between 0 and 10

This score suggests a very low level of positive thinking. You would do well to work on all or most of the categories in the table above. The following pages may help you to reflect upon your attitude in more detail. If you feel very poorly motivated, you may also find it helpful to talk to a student counsellor at college.

Reflection

In which areas are your scores highest? How can that help you?

In which areas are your scores lowest?

Which areas can you focus on, realistically, to improve your attitude?

Monitor your attitude: positive signs

It is worth monitoring your attitude from time to time in order to check that you are remaining motivated and likely to stay so. Our mood and our attitude can change without us really noticing. Over time, that can make it harder for us to catch the moment when we need to give our motivation a boost. Gentle monitoring of our attitude can help to check we are on track.

Positive signs

Identify which of the following are signs that you are likely to display when you are in a positive mood about your revision.

☐ I find I am keen to get down to study.

☐ There are times I notice that I am enjoying my study.

☐ I am keen to talk to other people about what I have learnt.

☐ I keep to my revision timetable – or study for longer than planned.

☐ I can remember a good proportion of what I have learnt, with few prompts.

☐ I display few signs of stress (see pp. 166–8).

☐ I am clear about my motivation for doing revision and exams.

☐ I don't notice the time go by when I am revising.

☐ I continue to think about aspects of my subject even when I am not revising.

☐ I feel I am using my time productively.

☐ I am able to put aside other activities in the short term, in order to study.

Reflection

How often do you notice these sorts of signs of positive approach?

How else do you display signs of a positive approach?

Getting in 'the zone' (ii)   49

Monitor your attitude: bad days

'Bad days'?

Despite good intentions, things can go wrong in the process of revision, and in the lead-up to exams. For example, we may get bored, lose confidence, or become discouraged by rumours about the exam or the examiners. It may take us longer to revise a subject than we had expected, or we find there are topics we need to cover that we hadn't planned on learning. It is useful to expect that there may be setbacks and bad days, and then plan how you will spot these and deal with them.

Warning signs

Consider which of the following are signs that you are likely to display when your motivation goes down.

☐ I find other things to do rather than study.

☐ I waste time when I sit down to revise.

☐ I finish my study sessions early.

☐ I feel dispirited or resentful at the idea of revising.

☐ I can't bear to look at my revision timetable.

☐ I can't remember much of what I have learnt.

☐ I become distracted by daydreams, doodling, and other time-wasting activities.

☐ I am always moaning and complaining to other people about work.

☐ I feel I am wasting a lot of time.

☐ I keep wanting to give up.

☐ I display several signs of stress (see pp. 166–8).

Attitude-monitoring strategy

I will monitor my attitude by:

☐ Keeping a journal and checking back over this each week.

☐ Asking a relative or friend to describe how I sound about revision or exams.

☐ Asking a relative or friend to point out to me when I am sounding negative or discouraged.

☐ Assigning a particular time of day when I will check my attitude to revision and exams in general.

☐ Other: give details.

Triggers for a negative attitude

Different conditions and circumstances can provoke a change in our attitude. If we are aware of those triggers that are likely to promote a negative response, we can be alert to these, and be more prepared to manage changes in our attitude before we lose our motivation. Circle those items below that are likely to trigger a change for the worse in your attitude to revision and exams. Then consider potential actions you can take to counter these triggers.

getting
bored with
revising

worrying about
letting other
people down

losing
faith in
myself

getting
overwhelmed
by how much
there is to learn

studying in
the evening

letting
myself get
discouraged by
rumours about
the exam

feeling
hungry

missing
my friends

putting too much
pressure on myself
to succeed

other (give
details)

other (give
details)

other (give details)

thinking about how
clever other people
are

dwelling on times
when I didn't do
as well as I had
wanted

other (give
details)

Managing your demons: Actions to counter negative triggers

	Negative trigger	Actions to counter the 'demons'
1	Getting bored with revising	● Break up revision into different activities of varying lengths of time. ● Set yourself a target to beat in order to provide more challenges, such as how many pages you will read, or reduce to shorter notes, by a specific time.
2	Worrying about letting other people down	● Provide a specific focus for each session of preparation time to prevent worry from serving as a distraction. ● Set yourself tasks for each 10–15-minute time slot. ● Focus on the benefits of achieving rather than the cost of failing.
3	Putting too much pressure on myself to succeed	● Focus on short-term tasks rather than thinking of long-term consequences. ● Read the sections on keeping exams in perspective (pp. 56–7).
4	Thinking about how clever other people are	● Remember that other people's strengths are irrelevant to how well you will do. ● Many aspects of what we consider 'clever' can be acquired over time and by practice.
5	Dwelling on times when I didn't do as well I as wanted	● If you know you do this, stop the train of thought as soon as you spot it, and focus on something different. ● Remind yourself of what you did do well. ● Focus on what you can do and have already learnt.
6	Feeling hungry	● Make sure you eat proper meals with slow-releasing carbohydrates and proteins, vegetables and fruit. ● Take breaks where you can have a snack. ● Study where you can nibble on fruit and snacks. ● Drink lots of water.

Managing your demons (*continued*)

	Negative trigger	Actions to counter the 'demons'
7	Getting overwhelmed by how much there is to learn	● Devise a sensible revision timetable and keep to it (see p. 107). ● As part of your revision timetable, break your subject up into themes and sections. ● Don't learn more than you need to: remember that you need to be selective. ● Cover a few subjects from all angles, rather than many subjects in a shallow way.
8	Letting myself get discouraged by rumours about the exam	● Some people set out deliberately to 'psyche out the opposition' by playing on their worries. Stay away from people who spread negative rumours about exams, and if you hear such rumours, dismiss them. ● Read the section on exam myths (pp. 64–75).
9	Losing faith in myself	● Talk to people you trust and who make you feel good about yourself. ● Focus on activities that will increase the likelihood of success rather than dwelling on what might happen. ● Draw up a list 50 things you can do – and put it where you can see it. ● Write out the most motivating thought you can think of on a 'good day', and put this where you will see it easily every day.
10	Studying in the evening/day	● Check whether you find it easier, over time, to settle down to study if you build a routine of studying at the same time, or whether you are more effective if you vary your study times. ● If you like to keep a particular time of day free, build in some days when you can spend that time the way you prefer. ● Check whether you use your revision time more effectively if you study at particular times of day or night.

Triggers for a positive attitude

Some circumstances and conditions are more likely to promote a positive attitude to revision and exams. It is best to note these on a 'good day', and to look back at them on days when revision seems tougher. First, identify those positive triggers that work for you; then consider ways of ensuring those triggers are easy to access and activate. Start by circling those items below that are likely to trigger a positive change in your attitude to revision and exams.

Remembering times I did better than I expected

Recognising aspects of my exam performance that I have improved

Thinking through how much I have already learnt

Taking pleasure in knowing the subject

Rewarding myself for completing stages in my revision

Revising with other people

Thinking about what I'll do after the exam

Imagining myself writing an answer well in an exam

Considering how much I will gain by passing

Finding a point of interest in every subject

Thinking I won't ever have to revise this again if I pass

Imagining myself hearing the news that I have passed well

Recognising my growing expertise

Positive triggers and rewards

Look back at the positive triggers you identified on the previous page. Consider how you can build these into your revision sessions, days and weeks.

Interim rewards

Some people motivate themselves to study by building in appropriate rewards at key stages in their revision schedule. Rewards may vary between, for example:

- having a break or snack only after a certain time spent revising or when a particular aspect of revision is complete;
- leaving the more interesting topics and revision activities until the more dutiful aspects are complete;

- organising activities in the evenings or at regular periods during the revision time, to create a proper break from revision;
- writing a list of books, CDs and DVDs to look at once the exams are over;
- planning a party or holiday after the exam.

Deferred gratification

People who do well at exams tend to be good at deferring gratification. In other words, they are able to focus on their main goal even if they don't enjoy the work in achieving it. They put off rewards and spending time as they would really like to in the short term, in anticipation of what this might bring them in the longer term. If you can keep the long-term gains of revision in mind, it is then easier to plan how you will remain motivated until the goal is achieved.

Finding inherent reward

The most effective attitude to 'reward' appears to be that gained by performing a task for the sake of it, rather than for external rewards. If this doesn't come naturally, then it can help to think creatively about:

- where is the intrinsic interest in the subject;
- how knowledge of the topic could help understanding of other subjects;
- where you could use the information in the future.

Keep exams in perspective (1)

Doing well at exams can depend on finding a healthy balance between maintaining very high levels of motivation on the one hand and, on the other, maintaining a realistic perspective on the importance of exams. Although high marks are usually linked to long hours, hard work and a strong drive to succeed, it is essential not to lose sight of the bigger picture and the everyday world beyond college and exams.

Importance of exams	Balance: keep exams in perspective
Exams are important to getting a degree.	Health, happiness, friends, family and a sense of well-being are more important in the bigger picture.
Exams measure success in an academic context.	Exams are not the only measurement of academic success: understanding the material and knowing how to apply it appropriately are more important.
Exams indicate what you have learnt.	Exam passes are not the same as having understood what you need to learn.
Exams contribute to improved life chances.	There is not an exact correlation between exam success and long-term career outcomes and a high salary.
Exams bring a sense of achievement.	Passing exams, and even gaining a degree, don't of themselves bring happiness, health and well-being.
Exams reflect courage, endurance and the ability to take on hurdles.	Taking exams indicates these things; passing exams with a particular mark does not.
Exams develop transferable skills such as time management and working under pressure.	Although exam success usually means putting in a lot of time and effort, it is essential to ensure that you sleep, take breaks, find some enjoyment in the day, and generally maintain your physical and mental well-being. Excessively long hours are not usually beneficial and can be counter-productive.

Keep exams in perspective (2): Touch base

- Circle all the items below that are important in your life apart from exams.
- Add in others that are important to you.
- Keep returning to this page to 'touch base' if you start to feel you are getting exams out of perspective.

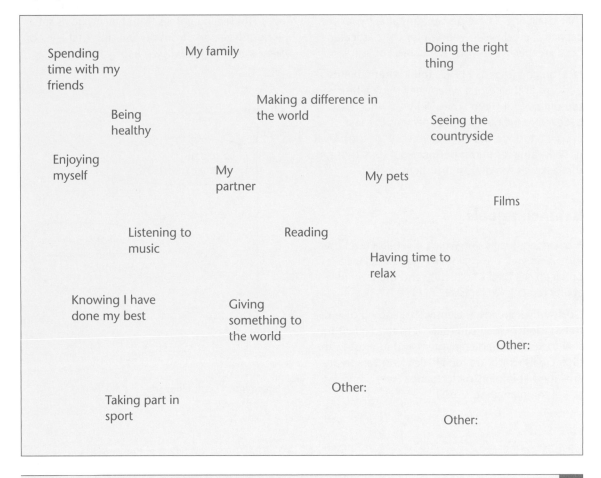

Spending time with my friends

My family

Doing the right thing

Being healthy

Making a difference in the world

Seeing the countryside

Enjoying myself

My partner

My pets

Films

Listening to music

Reading

Having time to relax

Knowing I have done my best

Giving something to the world

Other:

Taking part in sport

Other:

Other:

Self-belief and balanced goals

Perception and belief

You are more likely to attain peak performance in an activity when your perception of the challenge matches your perception of your ability to meet that challenge. These perceptions affect your capacity to believe in yourself for the particular task, irrespective of your actual level of skill.

Jackson and Roberts (1992) found that athletes perform at their worst when they think a task is too difficult for them. They did best when they believed in their ability to cope with the task. Even if a task should have been easy for their level of skills, athletes under-performed if they thought the task was too difficult for them.

Balanced goals

A balanced goal is one which is set at a level that motivates you, but maintains a good balance between the level of difficulty and the level of ability to achieve the goal.

Goals which are insufficiently challenging give rise to boredom, which can make it more difficult to stay focused or find enjoyment and interest in the task. Goals which are too challenging can create anxiety that impairs performance (see p. 169 on managing stress).

Ideal Performance State

Hardy, Jones and Gould (1996) use the term 'Ideal Performance State' to refer to the positive feeling that athletes gain from a sense of performing 'in flow'. This feeling comes from having goals set at the right level, and from recognising that level of balance as one that will work for you.

(Adapted from Hardy, Jones and Gould, 1996)

Realistic goals (1)

You are more likely to perceive a task as achievable if your goals are realistic. This means setting goals you believe are challenging but attainable. When taking exams, there are different levels of achievement that represent peak performance for individuals, as listed in the table below.

Goal A Which goal is achievable but still challenging for you? (tick one)	Reason Give your reasons for setting your goal at this level.
1 Just to turn up for an exam ☐ 2 To finish the exam paper ☐ 3 Near pass plus exam resit ☐ 4 Minimum pass ☐ 5 Comfortable pass ☐ 6 Good exam grades ☐ 7 Very good exam grades ☐ 8 Excellent exam grades ☐	

Goal B Which goal is achievable but still challenging for you? (tick one)	Reason Give your reasons for setting your goal at this level.
1 Good preparation for the exam ☐ 2 Answering the required number of questions ☐ 3 Giving reasonable answers ☐ 4 Giving at least one good answer ☐ 5 Giving several good answers ☐ 6 Giving only good answers ☐ 7 Giving very good exam answers ☐ 8 Giving only excellent answers ☐	

Realistic goals (2)

Out of 10?

Give yourself a rating out of 10 for the likelihood of achieving the goals you set yourself on p. 59.

Rating: 10 is very likely and 0 is not achievable.

0   1   2   3   4   5   6   7   8   9   10

Consider the rating you gave yourself. If it is low, then consider why this is the case. Is this because you doubt your ability, or are there other reasons?

Reflection

1   Are you setting your goals at levels which are likely to be too easy or too difficult?

2   What would need to be different to achieve the next level of challenge on the tables on p. 59?

3   Complete the table below. Then, consider whether the levels of stress and effort you have indicated are sufficient, too little, or too great to achieve the goal you would really like to achieve.

Whether your goal is realistic depends also on the levels of stress and effort you are willing to experience. You can use the chart below to consider the highest level of achievement you feel is possible when matched to the levels of stress and effort you are willing to undergo. Tick against the appropriate box in each column of the table below.

Goal		Level of stress		Level of effort	
Just to turn up for an exam	☐	No stress	☐	No effort	☐
To finish the exam paper	☐	Very little stress	☐	Very little effort	☐
Near pass plus exam resit	☐	Some stress	☐	Some effort	☐
Minimum pass	☐	Moderate stress	☐	Moderate effort	☐
Comfortable pass	☐	Quite a bit of stress	☐	Quite a bit of effort	☐
Good exam grades	☐	A great deal of stress	☐	A great deal of effort	☐
Very good exam grades	☐	Very high levels of stress	☐	Very high levels of effort	☐
Excellent exam grades	☐	Extreme stress	☐	Extreme effort	☐

Motivational goal (*why*) v. immediate task (*how*)

Peak performance is associated with finding the right balance between the longer-term motivational goal and focus on the immediate task.

Most of us are familiar with the idea that goals are motivating. However, less attention is paid to the importance of finding motivation in what we have to do now. Without focus on the immediate task, our desired goals can remain vague and unattainable. In other words, our aims or our peak performance are achieved in the present and through what we do now, not by what we intend to do at some time in the future.

> *Our aims or our peak performance are achieved in the present and through what we do now, not by what we intend to do at some time in the future.*

The longer-term goal

The 'dream' is important as it provides:
- motivation and a sense of purpose;
- a reminder of why you are bothering at times when study seems difficult;
- an answer to the question 'Why?'

The immediate task

This is important to:
- get things done;
- complete steps essential to ultimate success;
- avoid feelings of helplessness;
- prevent you from feeling overwhelmed by the significance of the longer-term goal;
- answer the question 'How?'

Why v. how

Although it can help to recall the motivational goal from time to time, thinking about the end point can be a distraction from what you need to do on a day-by-day basis. At critical points, it can be overwhelming and even sap your confidence to think about being 'the best' or 'perfect', gaining a first or achieving the highest marks.

Once you have a plan for achieving your peak performance, it is better to focus on completing that. Thinking about everything you have to revise can make it seem impossible to be ready for your exams. Focus instead on what you have planned for today, how you will revise, and how you will maintain your attention. It is then more likely that you will achieve.

Similarly, in the exam room, or at the start of a competition or just before going on stage, it is better to focus on how you will complete well the immediate tasks and interim steps rather than to think too much about what you want to achieve overall.

Closing comments

Summary Key points

★ Taking charge of your own attitude helps you develop towards peak performance.

★ Develop a fine-tuned awareness of your mental attitude.

★ Be aware of how exams affect you.

★ Identify your own negative triggers and 'demons' so you can manage them.

★ Identify your own positive triggers so you can mobilise them to motivate yourself.

★ Remain grounded: keep exams in perspective and be realistic in your goals.

★ Remain rooted in the here and now.

Having the right attitude to exams is an asset, and is one which can be developed by anyone. If you don't naturally take a positive approach to exams, and if you are not happy with your exam performance, then it may be time to take charge of your attitude and make it work for you.

The right attitude doesn't form in a vacuum. If you know you are well prepared for an exam in other ways, then it is likely that you will find it easier to be in a positive frame of mind. You may experience 'good days' when it is easier to feel positive. On such days, it is important to note your positive feelings and to make the most of them. It makes a great difference to your exam preparation and your performance in exams if you feel you can take charge of your attitude when you need to.

If you skipped Chapter 3 'Getting in "the zone" (i): Planning for peak performance', you may find it helpful to return to this now, and use it to plan more systematically towards achieving your best possible exam results.

Chapter 5

Exam myths and realities

Learning outcomes

This chapter supports you in:

- demystifying the exam process
- understanding how to interpret rumours about exams – and why these arise
- gaining a clearer understanding of the variety of ways in which people approach exams
- developing and maintaining your confidence in the face of potential attempts to unsettle you
- identifying unhelpful attitudes and strategies, so that you can avoid these
- identifying approaches for particular aspects of exam strategy

The '5-point plan for peak performance' (p. 41) identifies understanding exams and the examiner as part of what you need to know in order to feel confident about exam success. Demystifying the exam process is an important part of building a sounder knowledge of the challenge before you.

Exams tend to generate myths. These can arise for different reasons. Some are generated because students are unwilling to say how much work they are doing – and prefer other people to think their results were achieved without effort. If they fail, they can then say they didn't really try. If they succeed, people will be more impressed.

It can also feel as if we are walking into the dark as we approach an exam, because we don't know for certain what the questions will be, nor how we will react on the day. At times, this can make us feel as if we have little control over the outcome. This, in turn, can make us more susceptible to rumours, and more likely to grasp at straws. Even if we know that something is likely to be a myth, we may not feel we know for sure, and that can make us feel uncertain about what we can or can't, should or shouldn't, be doing in the lead-up to exams.

As there is often a grain of truth to a myth, that can also distort our perspective, especially when we are feeling unsure about what to believe. This chapter puts some common myths into perspective, and makes suggestions about ways you can take action where there are aspects of a myth that hold an element of truth.

Myths

Consider the myths listed below, and identify any that have concerned you. Each myth is considered in more detail in the following pages.

1　Other students are 'naturally good at exams' ☐

2　Other people don't mind exams ☐

3　Everyone hates exams ☐

4　Professor X always fails half of his students ☐

5　Exams are the most important aspect of the programme ☐

6　If I fail exams, this proves I am stupid ☐

7　Other students are not doing any revision yet ☐

8　You can prepare too much for exams ☐

　© Stella Cottrell (2006, 2012) *The Exam Skills Handbook*, Palgrave Macmillan

Myths (*continued*)

9 If you have a bad memory, you fail exams

☐

10 Exams only measure how fast you write

☐

11 If I write one really good answer, I can then answer fewer questions.

☐

Are you susceptible to exam myths and rumours? Are you able to ignore these or do they worry you?

How do you deal with such myths or rumours about forthcoming exams?

Do you have personal myths concerning your own performance? What are these? What will you do to address them?

Students' experiences

My sister said she was always watching TV in her room, and I thought it was amazing how she ever passed any of her exams. I felt she was the really bright one and I was a bit stupid next to her as I always work quite hard. Then I found out she just had the TV on in the background and was working away late into the night doing extra work. I don't know why she felt she had to hide it.

There is a gang of students at Uni who just like to make everyone worry. They are always saying things like how many students got kicked out last year for failing the exam. Last term, they said that the results for the previous year had been very high and the examiners were worried that they were making the exam too easy so they were going to set harder papers this year. They had made it all up and the exam paper wasn't harder, but some people got very worked up, very worried, beforehand.

It is like there is a competition between some courses to make out their subject is the hardest. If they say lots of people don't get through, or it's really hard to get good marks in their subject, then we are supposed to think they are more intelligent than us for getting onto such a difficult and prestigious course. You kind of know it isn't true, but then you hear other people talking about it as if it were true, and then you aren't so sure.

There is a student on our course who says he only ever writes one long essay for every paper. He always comes out near the top so it makes you think that could be a better way to do your exams. But then, you wonder, if the other good students did this as well, to get better marks like him, and if it wasn't true, then they would all fail, wouldn't they, and he'd look even better?

I think the younger students don't really worry about exams at all – they're so used to them after school. It's different for me. I have to prove myself to my kids and then, being older, it will look worse if I fail.

We have mature students on our course and they don't have to worry so much about impressing people because they already have life experience. They don't have the same pressures as us. When we leave, we only have our exam marks to fall back on. It's not like they have parents breathing down their necks all the time.

I heard that, one year, they just changed the exam format at the last minute because someone had stolen the exam paper. We didn't know what this meant exactly, and couldn't find anything out. We were all so worried – and it wasn't even true in the end.

Myth 1: Other students are 'naturally good at exams'

Natural ability

In areas such as sport, although there is recognition of the talent that people bring to their fields, there is also the assumption that talent is not enough. As national reputations can rest on medal success, a great deal of money and time is spent on developing the right psychological approach and physiological conditions to ensure that top athletes are able to gain an edge on other competitors.

Traditionally, exam success has been regarded in a very different light from athletic success. Good marks in academic subjects have been taken as a signal of intelligence, and as intelligence is believed to be an inherent ability, few people have used psychological and tactical approaches to boost their chances of success.

Research supports very different conclusions on how much intelligence is really inherent as a 'natural ability', and how far it is the result of external circumstances. However, common sense suggests that there are behaviours, actions and ways of thinking that are more likely to lead to success or to failure.

Strategies that anyone can access

Very few people who succeed at exams consistently do so through natural ability – hard work, effective strategies and strong motivation are much more likely causes. A large part of the success of your fellow students can be attributed to factors that are well within the control of yourself and others. These factors include:

- systematic preparation and practice,
- sufficient time spent in study, used effectively,
- self-belief.

Myth 2: Other people don't mind exams

Often, students prepare for exams on their own, so it is easy to imagine that everyone else is coping much better than they are. In reality, during the lead-up to exams, there are whole communities of students going through very similar experiences. Most have times when they feel:

- anxious about doing badly;
- regret that they didn't start revising earlier;
- bored with revising;
- despair of ever completing all there is to learn;
- worried that they are wasting time and avoiding getting down to revision;
- anxious that they won't remember what they have learnt;
- concerned that there are things they can't remember ever covering in class, or that they have missed out essential topics;
- despondent that they have spent hours reading without remembering anything.

If you are someone who finds exams difficult or unpleasant, be assured that you are not alone. At some point, most of us will have dreaded an approaching exam, wondering how we would ever get through and wishing we could be transported anywhere else in order to avoid it. Even those who are successful at exams don't necessarily enjoy them, and are not always efficient in using their time or managing their anxiety.

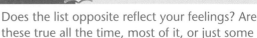

Reflection

Does the list opposite reflect your feelings? Are these true all the time, most of it, or just some of it?

Do you tend to assume other people are coping better than you are?

Hurray – exams! We love them

I can't wait

Myth 3: Everyone hates exams

This isn't true. Only some people do.

It is not unusual for students to dread the approach of exams, and there are certainly many people who do hate them. However, students approach exams in a range of ways. For example, they may:

- really enjoy the challenge;
- look forward to an opportunity to show off how much they know;
- enjoy some aspects of exams, such as the feeling of mastering a difficult subject;
- prefer exams to coursework;
- appreciate the anonymous marking;
- be glad of the exam as it means the course is nearly over.

There is no advantage in hating exams. The energy that goes into thinking negatively about them can be better directed into exam preparation. It is more constructive to:

- focus on positive aspects of exams (p. 20);
- spend time productively on preparation rather than wasting it in worry, such as through using structured revision sessions (Chapter 9);
- take steps to reduce the 'fear of the unknown' aspect of exams, through practising exam questions and mock exams;
- take control of your anxiety through stress management and through developing mental calm (see Chapter 10);
- work on a positive attitude and on understanding why this is so important to your success (pp. 54–5);

- set yourself challenges so you get a sense of achievement with each revision session.

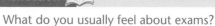

Reflection

What do you usually feel about exams?

How could you approach exams differently in order to feel better about them?

Myth 4: Professor X always fails half of his students

It is highly unlikely that teaching staff would systematically fail a large proportion of their students, as:

- academic staff usually want their students to do well;
- it reflects badly on their own teaching if a high proportion of their students fail;
- students pass if they meet the marking criteria;
- a large failure rate would be identified by the college's quality assurance processes, and the relevant academic staff would need to explain the cause; it is likely they would be asked to provide better teaching and support for students, to give them a more reasonable chance of success;
- external examiners are likely to query high fail rates and recommend changes in teaching, assessment or feedback.

Why do such myths arise?

Students can generate myths for various reasons such as:

- Setting a limit on how many students can pass makes the course seem more difficult, which makes those who are confident about passing feel they are particularly clever.
- If you think that only a small number are going to pass, this can provide an excuse for not

working, and for encouraging other students not to bother working either.

- If you can make other students lose their self-confidence, they may under-perform, so that your own answers then don't stand out as weak. This is sometimes referred to as 'psyching out' other students.
- Talking about worrying matters provides an outlet for personal anxiety, even though it may make other people anxious in the process.

he passes, he passes not, she passes, she passes not, she passes, . . .

Myth 5: Exams are the most important aspect of the programme

Although exams may be an important part of your course assessment, they are not necessarily the most important.

Other aspects are just as important

Exams are only one aspect of study: understanding the subject, developing your knowledge and thinking abilities, and developing broader skills that you can transfer to life and your career are usually considered just as important, if not more so. Most courses now require you to succeed in coursework and at demonstrating 'soft skills' such as teamwork.

High marks don't ensure success

High marks in exams may please you in the short term, but they are unlikely to add substantially to your life opportunities, career options or long-term happiness. People with relatively poor exam grades can do as well, or better, once they leave university.

Balanced approach

It is also important to maintain a balanced approach so that you are motivated to succeed without putting undue pressure on yourself. See p. 56 about keeping exams in perspective.

Reflection

Which aspects of your programme are most important to you?

How high a value do you attribute to good exam marks?

Myth 6: If I fail my exams, this proves I am stupid

Exams provide an objective way of assessing what you have learnt. However, they only test the kind of knowledge and understanding that lends itself to being examined. Some forms of intelligence, such as creativity, social skills and aspects of emotional intelligence, don't lend themselves to easy measurement or examination. That may be true of the areas where you excel.

Expect success

Most students do pass their exams and do well, even though they don't all expect to. The probability is that, if you avoid complacency, remain calm, and prepare sensibly for your exams, you will pass and do reasonably well.

Why does anyone fail?

There can be all sorts of reasons why people fail exams, and even why they could be expected to fail when, in practice, they pass. These reasons include:

- studying at too high a level, without having mastered basic levels first;
- lack of systematic preparation and poor memory joggers;
- lack of practice in taking exams;
- external life stresses;
- 'silly mistakes', such as misreading questions

or not checking for additional questions on the back of the paper;
- poor strategies for managing stress;
- not answering the right number of questions;
- not applying common-sense techniques, such as managing exam time appropriately;
- not reading sufficiently around the subject.

'Am I the only one who worries like this?'

If you worry about what your exam performance says about you, then you are not alone. Many students have unrealistic concerns that they will be 'found out' as unintelligent at any moment. Such thoughts are more likely to bring about failure than success. It is better to focus your attention on how you will pass rather than dwelling on negative thoughts: see Chapter 3, 'Getting in "the zone" (i)'.

'Maybe some people just can't do exams'

People with some disabilities can find it harder to do certain types of exams, and alternative arrangements are usually made for them (see pp. 255–6). Otherwise, with the right training, approaches and practice, anyone studying at the right level can pass their exams.

Myth 7: Other students are not doing any revision yet

Take an independent approach

It is important not to rely too much on other students' reports of what they are revising or not revising. For example, if someone tries to argue that there is no need to revise a particular subject, you must weigh up for yourself what you would gain or lose from revising it. It doesn't matter what other students are doing, you must revise what you need in order to achieve your objectives.

A common pretence

It is very common for students to pretend they are doing no work, or that they haven't started revising even close to the exam. Students will say they were out partying when they were really at home revising. In some cases, this is about 'image', for students who do not want to seem 'uncool' by appearing to spend their time in study rather than in going to clubs or pubs and seeing bands.

Some people exaggerate how little they are revising as a face-saving exercise. They hope that, if they fail, everyone will assume it was because they did no work and not because they couldn't have passed well if they had tried.

Other people say they have done no work as a form of self-promotion. They would like to

be regarded as 'brilliant' when they pass the exams well. They assume people will remember and comment upon how well they achieved on the basis of very little work. Yet other students feel they will do better themselves if they can convince other students not to revise. If everyone's marks are low, the paper may need to be marked differently or, at least, it might not seem so bad if many people fail.

Yeah – I'm out at this great party. Food, drink, it's crazy here. Can't hear a thing. I'll catch up with you tomorrow.

It is best to avoid discussing how much or how little revision you are doing, so that you don't make yourself or other students anxious.

Myth 8: You can prepare too much for exams

It is unlikely that you could do too much preparation. The right level of preparation leaves you:

- knowledgeable about, and still interested and engaged in, your subject;
- confident about recalling what you need;
- keen to demonstrate your understanding;
- calm but interested in the exam;
- competent at producing responses that are individual and relevant, at speed;
- balanced in your approach to other aspects of your life.

However, you can do too much of some kinds of preparation.

Too much information

It is possible to revise too much information on each subject. If you are good at selecting what you need, at speed, then this isn't a difficulty: you will just be very knowledgeable. However, if you find it difficult to decide quickly what to include when there is a word limit or a time limit, then it is worth using early preparation time to consider:

- What are the absolute essentials you need to know on each topic?
- What other information is likely to be very useful?
- Which details could add flavour to your answers, or make them stand out as different from everyone else's?

- How can you present this information as succinctly as possible?
- What might you like to include but it is highly unlikely you would be able to? It is useful to enter the exam knowing what you may need to omit, depending on the wording of the questions.

Too much of the same activity

People often do too much of the same kind of revision, such as:

- reading through their notes;
- memorising information;
- going over the same topics time after time, without bringing any variety or interest to the activity.

Too narrow an approach

You can also do too much preparation which focuses on:

- learning the content of the subject, at the expense of considering its significance, and how you will use it and when;
- revision, rather than other aspects of preparation such as maintaining your levels of interest, stamina and calm.

Other myths

Myth 9: If you have a bad memory, you fail exams

Passing exams is about much more than memory. Although we need to recall course material in order to pass exams, there are ways of working with information that make it easier to remember. Even if you feel your memory is poor, your memory efficiency is not a static entity as you can take steps to improve it: see Chapter 8.

Worrying about your memory can make it worse, as our ability to recall is sensitive to stress. Some excitement can help us to focus and think clearly, but anxiety can make it hard to think clearly or even to remember material we know well. Strategies for developing and maintaining calm assist exam memory.

Myth 10: Exams only measure how fast you write

This isn't true. Examiners don't want to read answers that are unnecessarily long. They set questions in such a way that you should be able to complete them in the time given, but you may be disadvantaged if your writing is slow. If this is the case, and you feel your handwriting is particularly slow, then you can benefit from speed writing regularly as part of your exam preparation.

If you can write quickly, this gives you an advantage in the time you have available to reflect, structure your answers, add interesting details, and check over your paper. If you are concerned about your writing speed:

- find a pen that you find easy to use for long periods of time;
- practise writing answers at speed;
- look for ways of phrasing information that is clear and precise, but brief and succinct;
- practise writing introductions and conclusions that are brief and to the point for essay-based exams.

Myth 11: If I write a really good answer, I can then answer fewer questions

This is not true. Always aim to produce the required number of answers, as it is normally easier to gain the marks needed for at least a basic pass. If you feel you don't have a good final answer, aim for the best final answer you can. Consider:

- whether there are any questions on the paper where you have a grasp of at least the basics;
- which material might start coming back to you if you start writing;
- whether you can answer at least part of a question.

Closing comments

Summary   Key points

★ Don't let exam myths distort your perspective.

★ Good strategy is more likely to lead to success than 'natural ability'.

★ Few people start out loving exams – but you can train yourself to do so.

★ Avoid getting caught up in assumptions about what other students are doing – focus on you.

★ Focus on action you can take to develop exam skills – avoid worrying about what might or might not happen.

We saw in Chapters 3 and 4 that taking charge of your attitude is a key ingredient of exam success. It is easier to take such control if we feel confident about the nature of the challenge before us and what is expected of us.

Exam myths can be very powerful in undermining our confidence or in setting up expectations that may not be borne out in reality. If you find yourself giving credence to rumours that may be untrue, stop and consider where these may have originated and whose interests they serve. In particular, consider how they are affecting your own attitudes and preparation for exams, and whether they are leaving you with a sense of reduced control over the exam outcomes.

If you want to do well in your exams, maintain attention on what you feel you need to do, plan accordingly, and stick to your plan. Don't measure your progress against what other people are doing. What works for them may not be right for you. Don't let others deflect you from your plan.

If you feel there is a grain of truth to the myth, such as whether writing speed has an effect on exam outcomes, then identify precisely where the reality lies, and consider whether it has any relevance for you. If it does, then your next step is to find a strategy to overcome any barriers it might set up, or to consider how you can use it to your advantage.

Because most students have not been in the role of an examiner themselves, a distinct set of myths can arise about what examiners do and don't do, what they want and don't want. This can feel confusing, especially if you have not taken many exams recently or have not done well in them. The following chapter focuses on giving you a better understanding of what examiners really want.

Chapter 6

What are examiners looking for?

Learning outcomes

This chapter supports you in:
- demystifying the exam process
- understanding how examiners mark exam answers and allocate marks
- considering the implications for your own exam strategy
- recognising characteristics of good exam answers
- understanding the words used in exam questions
- interpreting exam questions

In the lead-up to exams, students tend to ask 'What exactly do the examiners want?' Understanding what is expected of you forms an important part of the 'Know it!' and 'See it!' aspects of the '5-point plan for peak performance' (p. 41).

You can feel more confident about your exam preparation if you have a sense of what examiners do and the ways they are likely to approach the marking of your work. For example, by understanding what examiners are looking for when they choose particular words for an exam question, you are better placed to interpret questions in the manner they intended.

Although the process of marking exam papers varies from one examiner to another, exam boards or college regulations set limits on how far examiners can take an individual approach to marking. Despite this, myths can develop about what examiners are like, what they do, and the ways they would respond to different kinds of answer.

It is also useful to know the features that characterise good answers. You can then check whether your own answers demonstrate those features, and practise producing better answers before your exams.

Dispelling myths about examiners

Myth	Actuality
Examiners want you to fail	This is not true. Most students pass their exams in higher education. Examiners are monitored by second markers, external examiners and others, and if they were failing an unusual number of people, they would have to provide convincing explanations.
Examiners are eager to see what you don't know	This is not true. Examiners normally use a set of criteria to mark exam answers. It is more likely that they will be looking, actively, for where they can give your work marks for meeting each of those criteria.
Exam questions are worded in complicated ways in order to make the exam more difficult	This is not usually true. Exam questions are usually worded very precisely in order to help you understand exactly what is required. This is designed to help you interpret questions in the way the examiners intended.
Examiners want to see you have covered every aspect of the subject	Examiners don't want students to write down everything they know in an exam. They do want to see an intelligent selection of relevant information, applied to the specific question set. As they are expecting you to be selective, they cannot expect you to cover every aspect of your subject – not all of this would be relevant to the question. They also know that exam time is limited, so won't expect you to include the same level of detail as for a coursework answer.
Examiners will be able to tell all the things you haven't learnt and will give you low marks if they suspect there are areas you don't know about	If you provide an appropriate answer to the questions set, you will be awarded marks accordingly. Examiners look at the information presented, and cannot guess at what you might or might not know. They do not expect you to present every known fact about the topic as part of your answer. This means you can do well even if you don't know everything there is to know, so long as you can answer the questions you have selected.

How do examiners mark exam answers?

How examiners mark	Implications for your exam strategy
Speed Examiners mark quickly: they usually have a lot of scripts to mark.	Make sure your important points are clearly signposted so the examiner doesn't miss any. For example, for essay-based exams, clarify your position in your introduction and sum up, in your conclusion, how you have supported your argument. Make sure the first line of each paragraph introduces its main point clearly.
Marking criteria Examiners normally use a set of marking criteria: i.e. they will allocate marks for specific points and characteristics of answers, such as references to particular schools of thought, theories, or well-known research examples associated with the topic. They may allocate marks for more unusual but relevant examples, and for well-reasoned alternative interpretations of the evidence.	When preparing for the exam, give thought to which key points the examiner is likely to expect. Most of these will be fairly obvious from the main textbooks and journal articles for the subject, from lectures, and from the way the topic is normally broken down into sections. Organise these in a way that you can remember (see Chapter 8, on 'Memory').
Marking range Examiners do not always mark out of 100.	Different universities, or even schools within universities, use different marking scales. Although some universities do offer marks up to 100, it is more typical for 70 to be the highest mark awarded.
Marks per question Examiners will have maximum marks they can award for a question.	This means, for example, that if you are required to write three essays, a maximum of one-third of marks can be given for each. If you write only two answers, you cannot gain more than two-thirds of the marks. If the examiner's top mark is 70, then even two outstanding essays might only just scrape an overall pass of 46%. You gain higher marks from three reasonably good essays than two outstanding ones. For short answers, you will lose fewer marks for missing out a question, but you won't gain additional marks for long answers.
Marks per criterion/point Examiners will have maximum marks they can award for each point or for each of the various criteria.	This means that even if you have clever points to make, you should make them succinctly and move on to the next point. You are unlikely to gain extra marks by going into great detail on the same point, and are likely to lose marks if you don't include the expected basic information.

How examiners mark	Implications for your exam strategy
Expected characteristics of the answer Examiners will award or subtract marks depending on how far your answers meet the expected characteristics, such as those listed on p. 87.	Practising exam answers, and analysing your answers, can help you to develop the skills of writing good answers at speed. See p. 87 and Chapter 9.
Answers to specific questions Examiners are looking for answers to the specific questions you have selected. They are not interested in answers you may have written in the past for *similar* questions.	Avoid learning your current practice answers or coursework essays 'off by heart'. For essays, your answers are likely to answer the exam question more exactly if you work from a new plan, drawing on material you know well.
Only what is written down Examiners can mark only what you have written on the paper or exam book provided – not what you might have meant to say or include. They can't give marks for effort or whether you could have done better on a different day.	This means it is important to check your work carefully to make sure you have expressed yourself clearly. If your answer is muddled or you missed out essential words or details, examiners can't guess what you might have intended.
Can't read your mind Examiners aren't magical: they don't know what you don't know, which can be useful.	If you answer the set questions correctly, you receive good marks, even if you are completely ignorant about everything else on the course.
Anonymously and objectively Usually examiners do not know who wrote which script, so their marks should reflect the quality of the answer, not personal bias towards individuals.	You cannot rely on a good rapport with your lecturer, or your reputation as a student, to get better exam marks. Whether your lecturer does or doesn't like you shouldn't affect your marks.
Second and external marking Some or all exam scripts will be marked anonymously by a second marker and an external examiner to check for marking consistency.	You can generally be reassured that the mark you receive is appropriate, even if it was unexpected, as the examiner's marking will have been checked.

Managing the examiners

Although you can't directly influence the examiners, you can make an effort to ensure your exam script:

- creates a positive impression;
- avoids unnecessary irritations for the examiner;
- encourages the examiner to judge in your favour, if there is any room for giving the 'benefit of the doubt'.

Create a favourable impression

- Keep your exam papers or books clean, tidy and well organised.
- Number your answers correctly.
- Organise and structure your answers to respond to the questions you have selected.
- Select information: leave out material that is not required for this specific question.
- Don't try to prove how much you know.
- Avoid 'stream of consciousness' outpouring of everything you know, without selection or organisation: think 'quality' rather than 'quantity'.
- Avoid regurgitating the exact answers you have produced for coursework.
- Proofread your answers.
- Make any illegible words legible – don't assume the examiner will spend time trying to decipher your handwriting.

Don't write letters to the examiner

Dear examiner, I am sorry my exam paper is so messy. I had planned to write neatly but I got distracted from my best intentions. I am unusually tired today as people in my building arrived back late from the pub last night and set the fire alarm off, so I didn't get much sleep. I've also not been well recently and have had some personal and family problems, but I don't want to go into those now, I don't think my answers here reflect how well I could have done otherwise. I haven't had time to proofread the paper, so I hope you can guess what I meant. I really tried hard preparing for this exam, and deserve to do well so I hope you will take that into account too. I think my second answer is very good and hope you enjoy reading it as much as I enjoyed writing it. I hope you don't get too exhausted marking all these exam papers, and have a lovely summer holiday. Yours truly

Managing the examiners (*continued*)

Common irritations for examiners

The following features of exam scripts waste examiners' time. As examiners usually have only a few minutes to check whether your answers meet the exam criteria, it is not in your interests to waste that time. Put yourself into the shoes of an examiner, who may have dozens, if not hundreds, of scripts to mark, and imagine how you would react to finding scripts with some or all of these features:

- exam answers that are wrongly numbered;
- lack of clarity about which question the student is responding to;
- handwriting that is hard to read;
- important information lost amongst irrelevant narrative;
- a letter to the examiner trying to persuade them to take matters into consideration;
- messy scribble and blots, so that pages are unpleasant to look at;
- answers written in abbreviations or 'txt' notes;
- rambling answers that lack a clear structure and argument;
- lots of rough notes that have not been scored out, and which may or may not be part of the answers.

Presentation tips

- DNT TXT XAMs.
- There is no need to write out the exam question – this just wastes time.
- Make your key points stand out through the quality of your argument, rather than using colour, CAPITALS, underlining, or exclamation marks!
- Score a line through any rough notes, plans, and workings out (unless you are told specifically not to do this).
- Make sure that it is clear where one question ends and the next question begins.
- Check whether you need to start each question on a new sheet. It is possible that each answer will be sent to a different examiner who has expertise in the particular topic.
- Legibility is important but don't worry if your writing isn't beautiful.

What makes a good exam answer?

There are many kinds of exam – and what constitutes a good answer for each will vary to some extent. However, some broad principles apply to all good exam answers.

1. It answers the question as set

The most important feature of any good exam answer is that it addresses the question as set. Although this may seem obvious, all too often exam answers fail to do this. Instead, they appear to answer completely different questions, go off at a tangent, omit sections, or take the question as a broad invitation to write down anything known on the topic.

Often, students interpret exam questions in too broad a sense, rather than attending to the exact wording and what that really means. Examiners tend to phrase each question carefully so that you have to apply just a selection of your potential knowledge to a particular problem or issue. Factual knowledge is often less important than demonstrating through your answer the critical and creative thought process you have used in addressing the problem or issues.

2. It meets the given criteria

On most programmes, there is little mystery about what kinds of answers gain good marks. Marking criteria are normally provided, giving details of what gains the best, average and low marks, or a fail.

Reflection **Using marking criteria**

Circle either *Yes* or *No*, as best applies to you.

I always read the marking criteria at the start of the programme. **Yes / No**

I always check that I understand what these mean, and ask if I am uncertain. **Yes / No**

I make use of the marking criteria when organising material for revision. **Yes / No**

I make use of the marking criteria when devising practice answers for my revision.
Yes / No

3. It includes all the expected basic points

Examiners will read your exam answer looking for an expected set of points that apply to that question, and which they expect all students on that course to know. A good answer must cover these as a basic minimum – though that alone doesn't make an answer good.

Reflection **Basic points**

Circle either *Yes* or *No*, as best applies to you.

I jot down a list of all the points that must be included for the set question, and then check each off as I cover it in my answer.
Yes / No

4. It includes only relevant material

All of the material you include in your answers should be relevant to the question or title. In practice, this means writing to the point and omitting extraneous material.

Reflection **Relevance in your exam answers**

Circle either *Yes* or *No*, as best applies to you.

Even when I know the topic well, I always consider carefully the particular angle or issues relevant to the specific exam question.
Yes / No

I take care to include only such information as is relevant to the angle of the question.
Yes / No

I am careful to omit material that is not relevant to the exam question. **Yes / No**

I practise adapting my material to suit different exam questions on that topic. **Yes / No**

What makes a good exam answer? (*continued*)

5. It is audience-aware

A good exam answer is one that shows excellent awareness of the 'audience', whether this is an actual audience, as for presentations, or just the examiner. This means that the answer:

- selects and presents information in such a way that it is always clear to the audience what is being said and why;
- is well structured, so that the audience can take in the information quickly and easily;
- provides interest, through taking an unusual angle or including less obvious examples, details, observations or critique.

> **Reflection** **Audience awareness**
>
> Circle either *Yes* or *No*, as best applies to you.
>
> I always provide a brief introduction, outlining my argument and stating why the issues inherent in the question are significant. **Yes / No**
>
> I organise my material, grouping related points together. **Yes / No**
>
> I link each point to the next so that there is a logical flow to my answers. **Yes / No**
>
> I prepare for the exam by considering interesting angles, examples and details.
> **Yes / No**

6. It shows a good grasp of the subject discipline

If you engage with your subject, reading and thinking about it, you can develop a feel for the discipline that then makes it easier to:

- recognise when exam questions refer to recent research articles or topical debates;
- recognise which material is significant and deserves most emphasis in your answer;
- anticipate which exam questions will be set, and the kind of answer expected.

> **Reflection** **Grasp of the discipline**
>
> Circle either *Yes* or *No*, as best applies to you.
>
> I read a lot of background material. **Yes / No**
>
> I think a lot about the subject. **Yes / No**
>
> I think through, for myself, the potential implications of developments in the subject.
> **Yes/No**
>
> I look for ways of using knowledge I gain in one area to help me understand other areas.
> **Yes /No**

> **Reflection** **Good answers**
>
> If you answer 'No' to any of the items on pp. 83–6, consider what, if anything, you could do differently next time.

7. It shows a sound understanding of concepts

Following on from 6 above, good exam answers demonstrate a solid understanding of core course concepts. They do more than simply provide grouped lists of well-learnt facts. Rather, they draw out such things as:

- the nature and significance of the relationships between different sets of information;
- why certain new approaches were ground-breaking at the time;
- the relevance of one theory to another;
- the significance of a series of research findings in advancing our understanding of an issue;
- why certain theories or approaches would be the most useful for addressing a given problem.

Reflection   Understanding of concepts

Circle either *Yes* or *No*, as best applies to you.
I spend time making connections between different aspects of my programme.
Yes / No

I spend time thinking through the significance of what I am learning – and how it could, or couldn't, apply to different contexts. **Yes / No**

I spend time finding out, and thinking about, why particular material is significant – or not.
Yes / No

8. It shows an unexpected 'spark'

The best answers contain a 'spark' that makes them stand out from the rest. Such answers demonstrate the strengths outlined in 1–7 above. They also tend to do one or more of the following:

- show an unusually good grasp of the material and its relevance to the issues;
- bring together diverse material well, and in unexpected ways that work;
- show evidence of deep thought rather than regurgitation from lectures and books;
- include good ideas that make the examiner pause and think.

Reflection   Spark

Circle either *Yes* or *No*, as best applies to you.

I spend a lot of time thinking about theories and ideas and how I could apply them in different ways. **Yes / No**

I read about other subject disciplines in order to look at my own from a new perspective.
Yes / No

I bring a critical eye to everything I read for my course. **Yes / No**

I am active in looking at ways of synthesising material so as to find new ways of looking at issues relevant to my programme. **Yes / No**

12 characteristics of good exam essays

A good exam essay:

1 **Answers the precise question set,** rather than presenting information that is broadly relevant to that topic.

2 **Has a clear argument or perspective,** so that the examiner knows from the outset what you intend to say, and can trace the development of your argument throughout the essay.

3 **Is critical and analytical,** engaging with debates in the subject, and explaining *why* something is significant, rather than simply describing *what* research there is or what theorists have said.

4 **Is structured**: includes a brief introduction, short paragraphs each dedicated to one key aspect of your argument, and a conclusion, all structured around the main argument.

5 **Provides reasons, based on sound evidence,** to support the main argument.

6 **Has good paragraphing**: the main point of each paragraph is introduced clearly, and paragraphs follow logically from each other.

7 **Evaluates different perspectives**: it weighs up the relative value or significance of different points of view or theories, evaluating the key arguments and evidence for these, and making it clear why one set of arguments, reasons or evidence is more convincing than others.

8 **Refers to theories and schools of thought** relevant to the question, demonstrating an understanding of the significance of these to the subject.

9 **Includes references**: where relevant, exact references (names and dates) for key theories and research articles are included.

10 **Is selective**: it includes just the information and detail that is most relevant to answering the question, and leaves out less relevant material.

11 **Is written clearly and to the point,** without waffle, repetition, grand generalisations, pompous language, unnecessary jargon, or personal anecdotes.

12 **Has been proofread** to make sure it makes sense, and says what you intended to say. Minor errors are removed and all words made legible.

Evaluation of your exam essays

Read through 2–3 essays you either completed as coursework or as practice answers in your revision sessions. Evaluate these using the 12 characteristics of a good essay.

Characteristics	Evaluation of my essays
1 My answers are highly focused on answering the questions exactly as set.	
2 My answers present arguments clearly.	
3 My answers include critical analysis of key debates, issues, theories or research.	
4 My answers are well structured.	
5 My answers provide reasons to support the main arguments, based on sound evidence.	
6 My answers are well paragraphed.	
7 My answers evaluate different perspectives.	
8 My answers refer to relevant theories and schools of thought.	
9 My answers include accurate references.	
10 My answers are selective, containing the most relevant information and details.	
11 My answers are written clearly and to the point.	
12 My answers have been proofread and are free of spelling errors, word omissions, etc.	

Words used in exam questions

These words indicate the approach or style expected for the piece of writing.

Account for   Give reasons for; explain why something happens.

Analyse   Examine in very close detail; identify important points and chief features.

Comment on   Identify and write about the main issues, giving your reactions based upon what you have read or heard in lectures. Avoid purely personal opinion.

Compare   Show how two or more things are similar. Indicate the relevance or consequences of these similarities.

Contrast   Set two or more items or arguments in opposition so as to draw out differences. Indicate whether the differences are significant. If appropriate, give reasons why one item or argument may be preferable.

Critically evaluate   Weigh arguments for and against something, assessing the strength of the evidence on both sides. Use criteria to guide your assessment of which opinions, theories, models or items are preferable.

Define   Give the exact meaning of. Where relevant, show that you understand why the definition may be contentious in the context of your subject.

Describe   Give the main characteristics or features of something, or outline the main events.

Discuss   Write about the most important aspects of (probably including criticism); give arguments for and against; consider the implications of.

Distinguish   Bring out the differences between two (possibly confusable) items.

Evaluate   Assess the worth, importance or usefulness of something, using evidence. There will probably be cases to be made both *for* and *against*.

Words used in exam questions (*continued*)

Examine	Put the subject 'under the microscope', looking at it in detail. If appropriate, 'Critically evaluate' it as well.
Explain	Make clear why something happens, or why something is the way it is.
Illustrate	Make something clear and explicit, giving examples or evidence.
Interpret	Give the meaning and relevance of data or other material presented.
Justify	Give evidence which supports an argument or idea; show why a decision or conclusions were made, considering objections that others might make.
Narrate	Concentrate on saying what happened, telling it as a story.
Outline	Give only the main points, showing the main structure.
Relate	Show similarities and connections between two or more things.
State	Give the main features, in very clear English (almost like a simple list but written in full sentences).
Summarise	Draw out the main points only (see 'Outline'), omitting details or examples.
To what extent	Consider how far something is true or contributes to a final outcome. Consider also ways in which the proposition is not true. (The answer is usually somewhere between 'completely' and 'not at all'.)
Trace	Follow the order of different stages in an event or process.

Interpreting exam questions

Although question words may vary in meaning in a dictionary sense, most exam questions are structured to require one of very few approaches. If you can recognise those approaches, then it is easier to feel confident that you could attempt any type of exam question. The right-hand column, below, indicates the general type of response required.

Interpreting exam questions	
1 **How significant?** Critically analyse; analyse; review the arguments for . . . Argue the case for . . .	Most questions are likely to require critical analysis of evidence or differing perspectives, even if this is not stated in the question. You need to consider the significance or quality of the evidence to support particular point(s) of view, including the evidence for opposing views, and provide a reasoned argument to show which is the most convincing evidence or set of arguments.
2 **How much?** To what extent? Evaluate . . . Assess how far . . .	Weigh up the arguments 'for' and 'against', and work out which way the evidence leans. This may mean asking: ● How effective is this? ● Does this evidence support the theory? ● Was this policy successful . . . ? ● What are the relative strengths and weaknesses? ● Is the evidence sufficient to prove the hypothesis? Such answers often require you to include critical analysis of different viewpoints, theories, evidence or arguments.
3 **Why . . . ?** Explain . . . Provide reasons for . . . Justify . . . Account for . . .	These sorts of questions require you to provide reasons for why something happens. Why did a particular outcome occur? However, consider whether there are different viewpoints on the reasons 'why'. If so, the question then needs critical analysis of the different perspectives and theories.

Interpreting exam questions	
4 **Why?** Discuss; explore; consider;	These sorts of questions may be vaguely worded, but generally require you to analyse critically different theories, evidence or points of view, as part of a reasoned argument based on evidence.
5 **What?** Describe; outline; state; trace. Provide an account of . . . Illustrate . . .	These sorts of questions are generally asking for informational details about an item or event, or to see if you can list all the steps in a sequence. These answers are usually descriptions, narratives of events, lists, or instructions written out in full. However, consider whether there are different viewpoints about any aspect. If so, include critical analysis of the different perspectives.
6 **Similarity/difference** Compare; contrast. What are the differences between . . . ?	These sorts of questions require you to weigh up possible conclusions where two or more items are similar or different, pros and cons, or arguments 'for' and 'against'. Such questions can be straightforward. However, you may need to include critical analysis of alternative viewpoints, such as the value or significance of any differences or similarities.

Critical analysis within exam questions

You can see from the table above that critical analysis plays an important role in many kinds of exam question, irrespective of the wording. In arts, humanities, languages and social sciences, critical analysis is often the aspect of an essay that carries the most marks. This means it is worth looking for natural opportunities to include critical analysis as part of your answer. For science and mathematical subjects, questions that require verbal discussions of findings also require the application of critical reasoning skills.

It is useful to spend time developing your skills in critical analysis and argument as part of your advance preparation for exams, in order to write stronger and clearer answers. For more on developing these skills, see Cottrell (2011).

The importance of 'However, . . . '

Exam answers generally gain strength from considering alternative viewpoints, often introduced by the word 'However, . . . '. As the chart below illustrates, answers may share similar features despite differences in the wording of the question. Exam essays tend to require features from each of the four columns, and may move back and forth between the 'However' and 'So what?' columns several times.

	(1) +	(2) –	(3) However,	(4) So what?
Type of essay	Give obvious points in favour/ pros, similarities, comparisons, strengths.	Give obvious points against/ cons, differences, contrasts, weaknesses.	Show alternative way(s) of looking at the subject, at the pros or cons, etc.	Evaluate the relative worth of each alternative viewpoint, making a judgement about its significance to your argument.
Critical analysis essays	Include points that support your position (arguments, reasons, evidence or examples).	There may be minor points to consider against your argument.	Raise alternative theories or schools of thought which challenge your main argument.	Consider the strengths and weaknesses of these alternative viewpoints, showing why they are not significant enough to overturn your main argument.
'Compare and contrast' or 'Evaluate points for and against . . . ' essays	Draw out similarities or points 'for'.	Draw out differences, or points 'against'.	Consider alternative viewpoints about the balance or significance of similarities and differences; points 'for' or 'against'.	Evaluate the significance of alternative viewpoints: do they enhance the similarities or the differences, or strengthen either the pros or the cons?
'To what extent?' essays, e.g.: To what extent was Lucas right that . . . ?'	Give standard reasons for believing Lucas was right to argue that . . .	Give standard reasons for believing Lucas was wrong to argue that . . .	Show alternative viewpoints about whether Lucas was right or wrong . . .	Evaluate the significance of alternative viewpoints, bringing out their relative strengths. Draw conclusions.

Closing comments

Summary Key points

★ Teaching staff want their students to succeed – this reflects well upon them too.

★ Understand the examiner's mind-set: mark, at speed, a past paper of your own or of a friend.

★ Be aware of how students lose marks unnecessarily.

★ For essay-based exams, apply the 12 characteristics of good essays.

★ Be aware of what makes a good answer in different kinds of exam.

★ Avoid typical exam errors – use common sense.

★ Reflect carefully on your own approaches to answering questions currently.

★ Make sure you know how to interpret exam questions.

Planning towards peak performance includes developing a strong mental image of how you will succeed. In order to do this, you need to gain as complete a picture as you can of every aspect of the exam process. This includes identifying what you can realistically expect of the examiner and the exam, and dispelling unhelpful myths.

You will probably feel better about your exams if you consider the examiner as more of an ally than as an enemy. Your examiners are likely to be looking to see where they can give you marks in line with their marking criteria, rather than looking for ways to take marks away. Give thought to the likely marking criteria for different types of question and how you would go about meeting these.

As part of your exam preparation, think through what key points are likely to gain marks for specific questions that have been set on past papers, and what other aspects of those questions might gain or lose marks. It is worth talking to your lecturers to investigate what else is valued in exam answers for your subject area.

Understanding how examiners work and what they are looking for means that you can plan your exam preparation time more effectively. For example, when you write practice answers, mark these yourself as if you were the examiner. Leave a few days and mark them again – you may find it is harder to make sense of what you have written once the answer starts to fade in your own mind. Consider how easy your answers are to read and whether the main points stand out clearly.

Finally, bear in mind that examiners have a difficult task, marking many papers in a short time, with hundreds of students each selecting from the same range of questions. Avoid adding to their work by writing illegible, confusing and rambling answers. Ensure that your paper stands out for answers that are clear, structured, interesting, legible and well argued.

Chapter 7

Revision strategies

Learning outcomes

This chapter supports you in:

- understanding what is meant by revision
- recognising common mistakes, to help you avoid these
- preparing a revision timetable
- identifying different ways of revising
- making revision a more interesting and enjoyable experience
- revising with other people

Revision can be either interesting or extremely dull, depending on how you approach it. It is such an essential part of exam preparation that the more effective, interesting and enjoyable you can make it, the better your chances of exam success. All five key aspects of the '5-point plan for peak performance' (p. 41) apply to revision.

At its best, revision can be an excellent way of deepening our learning, drawing together our knowledge and understanding. However, in practice, students tend to describe inefficient strategies that leave them bored, anxious and resentful of the time they are losing from their everyday lives.

We saw in earlier chapters that enjoyment is a characteristic of achieving peak performance. This is true, too, of time spent in revision. Part of your revision strategy should consist of identifying ways of bringing interest, enjoyment and challenge to each revision session. Start with a positive outlook about how you can make your revision productive and stimulating.

This chapter provides examples of revision strategies on which you can build to make your revision more effective, including guidance on revising with other people. It also presents common revision mistakes – so you can plan to avoid them.

What is revision?

Revision as a process

Revision is a process of revisiting course material that you have already covered, in order to:

- refresh your memory of it, reminding yourself of what you know so far;
- check that you understand what you have learnt;
- fill in gaps in your knowledge and understanding;
- reinterpret material in the light of other topics you have covered;
- reorganise information in order to make it useful for other purposes, such as recalling it for exams;
- test your recall of each topic, so that you can make use of your learning in exam conditions.

How do people revise?

People revise in very varied ways: with others or on their own, in long sessions or in short bursts, planned well in advance or attempted in a frantic rush, focused around reading notes or consisting of many different activities, in any kind of location.

It is not unusual for people to sit down to similar activity in each session, become bored and distracted, and end up frustrated at making little progress. On the other hand, revision can be a reassuring, and even an exciting process, as you:

- notice how much you have covered on the course;
- take charge of your exam preparation, giving yourself more control over the exam outcome;
- rediscover interesting material that you had forgotten about;
- realise you now understand material that had previously been confusing;
- appreciate how your subject fits together as a whole rather than the segments you covered on a week-by-week basis;
- identify topics that attract you the most;
- find ways of making sense of those areas you had previously found difficult;
- set yourself challenges that will help you to achieve your personal goals;
- recognise your growing expertise in the subject.

Long-term and short-term revision

Advantages of revising over time

Revision that builds over time is usually better than revision that starts shortly before the exam. Revising material from early in the course means:

- you are likely to be more relaxed when learning, so that it is easier to take in information and remember it;
- you recognise material more easily later on in your exam preparation, as you have been over it already;
- your later exam preparation feels more manageable, and there is less last-minute panic;
- going over material several times at intervals helps to build recall of it;
- you are more likely to see links between different topics if you are revising one subject, even in a general way, whilst learning a new subject;
- there is an increased chance that you will understand material that you found difficult the first time round, if you give the brain the opportunity to see it and mull it over;
- you have greater opportunities to develop a broad-based approach to revision, such as developing techniques for relaxation and managing stress, building your knowledge base, and developing good memory strategies.

The focus of long-term revision

It is not likely that you can revise all course material at regular intervals, as there simply wouldn't be time, and you may find that even interesting material starts to grow stale if you revisit it too often. However, if you do start preparing early for your exams, you can:

- use a structured programme to develop your knowledge and exam strategies (see Chapters 8, 9, 13 and 14);
- identify aspects that you find particularly difficult to understand or remember, and return to these for short revision sessions spread over a longer period.

Revising in the short term

Short-term revision is the revision you would normally do in the final 1–2 weeks before an exam. Ideally, it would be the culmination of a longer-term strategy. If you have left your revision very late, then see Chapter 12 for emergency measures that you can take.

Common mistakes in revision strategies

The table below lists poor revision strategies. Use the columns on the right to identify which are true of your own revision strategies.

Common mistakes	My revision ✔		
	Occasionally	Often	A lot
1 Leaving all revision until the last minute			
2 Finding there is always something more important to do than revise			
3 Spending too much time planning revision and too little time actually revising			
4 Working alone too much			
5 Meeting other people to revise but spending the time doing other things			
6 Avoiding revision because it is boring			
7 Reading, revising or making notes for some time and not being able to remember much about it			
8 Spending a long time on the same subject without feeling you are making progress			
9 Revising too few subjects			
10 Not being able to identify the really key points about each topic			
11 Revising too much information			

Avoiding common mistakes in revision

	Common mistake	Action to take
1	Leaving all revision until the last minute	• At the beginning of your programme, set a date for starting your revision. • Put this date into all diaries, planners and organisers that you use. Also, enter several reminders both before and after that date. • Ask someone that you trust to prompt you to get started. • Decide, well in advance, three things you will do in your first revision sessions (see p. 104). Write these into your diary or revision planner. • Choose a structured revision session to get started (p. 141).
2	Finding there is always something more important to do than revise	• Set yourself short revision sessions, leaving yourself the option to study for longer if you become engaged in the subject. • Timetable 10-minute slots at regular intervals into your diary in order to browse quickly through past exam papers, your notes and the syllabus. In that 10 minutes, jot down a quick list of what you will do in your next revision session. • If you are using distractions as an excuse not to revise, put time aside in your diary to do these at specific times before or after your revision. • Start each session with a few moments to remind yourself of your motivation for taking your programme of study.
3	Spending too much time planning revision and too little time actually revising	• Decide on a rough outline for your plan, focusing on when you will study and the general subject area. Write any details only in pencil – or produce your plan electronically so you can update it more easily. • If you tend to redesign your revision timetables several times, allow yourself a maximum of three versions. After that, work with whatever you have got, adapting it rather than starting it from scratch.

	Common mistake	Action to take
4	Working alone too much	It is fine to revise alone if you know this suits you best. Many people prefer this. However, if you feel you are spending too much time alone, consider working occasionally in the library or set up a study group (pp. 111–12).
5	Meeting other people to revise but spending the time doing other things	● Before you meet, agree start and end times, and decide the areas you will revise. ● Avoid mixing study with alcohol and main meals. ● Consider whether your study group has the right composition: should it split into two or add different members? ● Set ground rules for the group that you can all agree. If you don't think the group is working in helping you to revise, then consider leaving it.
6	Avoiding revision because it is boring	● Revision doesn't have to be boring, so consider how you can make your revision sessions more engaging (see pp. 108–10). ● Generally, varying what you do from one session to another will add interest. ● Setting specific tasks within a given timescale adds more challenge.
7	Reading, revising or making notes for some time and not being able to remember much about it	● This is usually a sign that you are not sufficiently involved with the task, because it is either repetitive, too routine, or not challenging your mind sufficiently. You are probably not engaging your mind in an inner dialogue with the subject. ● Break your revision sessions into smaller sections, with specific tasks to achieve by the end of each section. ● Check back at the end of each section to see what you have learnt. ● At regular intervals, spend three minutes jotting down what you have just been learning. Check this against your main notes. ● Avoid simply reading through your notes: do something that involves you in thinking about the information, such as devising a mnemonic (pp. 132–3) or using it in a structured revision session (p. 141).

Avoiding common mistakes in revision (continued)

	Common mistake	Action to take
8	Spending a long time on the same subject without feeling you are making progress	● Use a 'little and often' method – rather than trying to cover the subject in one session. ● Start with an overview, and return to the details in a future session. ● Look for ways of engaging your attention as you study, making your revision more interesting (pp. 108–13). ● Set specific goals for a session or series of sessions, so you can measure your progress. ● Also: use the methods listed for 7, above.
9	Revising too few subjects	● If you know this is a mistake, then you have almost solved the problem: plan your time so that you are able to revise more topics. Aim to give yourself the opportunity of some choice of questions in the exam. ● See 'How much is "enough"?' (pp. 105–6). ● See 'Structured revision sessions' (p. 141).
10	Not being able to identify the really key points about each topic	This is often a sign of not understanding the subject sufficiently well: you are unable to detect what is significant in relation to other material in the subject. ● Read more about your subject. Browse through several general books on the subject to gain an overview of the headings, topics and names that appear most often. ● Look at the index at the back of books and see which items are referred to the most – this should indicate the more important subjects. ● Note which items are referred to across several different areas of your subject. ● Find out whose work is regarded as 'seminal' – i.e., work regarded as a 'classic' for the subject or which generated major new lines of enquiry.
11	Revising too much information	● This can be useful if it gives you a good sense of the subject. However, it is worth spending time before the exam filtering out the detail that might have been useful for coursework but which you won't have time to refer to in the exam. See 'Structured revision sessions' (p. 141).

Students' experiences of revision

I work myself up to any study, including revision, by being on my own doing whatever I feel I need to do – eat, chill out, listen to music, whatever. I'm not avoiding revision – it's just how I psych myself up to do it. If I feel I am in control of my time, then I feel OK about studying once I get going.

I can't imagine anything worse than revising on your own. I have to do it sometimes but when I can, I meet up with my mates after seminars and we put in a few hours checking we all understand the lectures, or working on a difficult area together.

I have to 'nest' before I can revise. I tidy up, shop, spend time looking out of the window, thinking about nothing in particular as I settle down. I suppose you could say I am using time ineffectively, but I'm not sure about that. I actually enjoy revising – I just get focused in my own way.

I used to avoid revising with other people because I saw them as competition. When I came back to study after a few years away, I felt more relaxed about it. Now, I'd say I value the ideas that emerge when a group works together well. There's always something I take home that I wouldn't have arrived at on my own.

Studying with other people is so over-rated. So much time is wasted in travel, small talk, socialising. There's always someone who has to repeat what everyone else has said, and people who don't understand, and you end up carrying them.

I find groups often work to the lowest common denominator – and go much more slowly over the material than when I study on my own. Having said that, I have noticed that I remember much more easily the points that came up through discussion – so the time isn't really wasted.

I chewed through all my pens, my nails, even the end of my hair. I day-dreamed. I drank coffee. I watched TV. I had my folder on my knees and I doodled in the margins. I got really fed up, and definitely had too much caffeine. Some things did go into my head, but there has to be a better way.

I always check the syllabus at the beginning of the course and work out when we are covering each section through lectures. I use this as the basis of my revision timetable – I like to be methodical in making sure I have covered everything at least once.

Students' experiences of revision (*continued*)

Every day, I sat down to work at my schedule. I'd be doing really well and then my flatmate would come in and start asking if I was working too hard, if I needed anything, whether I could help her, whether I should be taking a break. She kept telling me about an aunt of hers who went prematurely grey because of too much study. I always ended up getting into an argument with her and then being too annoyed to focus on my work.

It was six weeks away from my Geography exam and I decided to look at some past papers. I noticed with horror that there were questions about volcanoes, weather maps and river systems. I didn't know anything about these. I would have been really shaken if I had got into the exam and seen lots of questions I couldn't answer: I thought we had covered everything we needed to know in class. It was only then that I looked at the syllabus and realised that there were loads of other things that I needed to know. I tried to work out how many questions I would have been able to answer from previous years' exams, and realised that I would have had no choice at all.

Reflection 📖 Revision

How do your experiences of revision compare with these students' (pp. 102–3)? Do their views change your opinions about the way you study?

Setting about revision

- Draw up a plan of what you intend to revise and when you will revise each major area.
- Organise your notes so you can find what you need easily and quickly. Label things well.
- Organise your environment so it suits your revision style (see p. 25).
- Monitor how you might be wasting time – such as through endless cups of coffee? Making phone calls? Suddenly deciding you need to tidy your room? Consider how you will avoid this.
- Consider how you might sabotage your own revision success – and have a plan to counteract this.

If you are not sure how to get started on a revision session, see the box opposite. Choose one or more of these activities to help you begin.

Getting started on revision

- Start anywhere rather than worrying where to start. For example, simply open any file or jot down an essay outline from memory – anything that starts to focus your attention on your exams. Your mind is then more likely to be inspired about what you can do next.

- Choose something easy for your first session so that you gain an early taste of success.

- Pick your favourite topic. Quickly write down as much as you can recall about it without stopping or checking.

- Write for 5 minutes on one topic that you vaguely recall. See whether more information returns to you as you write. Then, compare what you have written with the material in your notes.

- If you haven't a copy of the syllabus, acquire one as soon as you can. Read through it several times, comparing what it says with what you are likely to cover in lectures and seminars. There are often topics that you are expected to cover on your own rather than through the lecture and seminar series.

- Acquire copies of past exam papers. Compare the questions that appear in these with the subjects listed in the syllabus. Check, too, whether the style or pattern of questions has changed in recent past papers.

- Work through the first few structured revision sessions (p. 141).

How much is 'enough'? (1)

You have less time in an exam to cover a subject than you have for a coursework essay or seminar. This doesn't mean you have to write at superhuman speeds in order to cover the same ground. Your examiner will expect shorter answers, and wants to see that you can recognise the most significant information and be selective.

Identify the essentials

For each subject you decide to revise, find out:

- how the subject breaks down into key themes or topics;
- the main points of view, or schools of thought, on each topic;
- key debates in the subject over time;
- recent important debates;
- the *major* pieces of research for each topic, who conducted these and when, and the significance of the research;
- the *most recent* significant research on the subject and its relevance;
- which point of view you find most convincing and why.

Map it out

Draw a chart to draw together, for each theme:

- Key schools of thought on the theme.
- Themes covered by each key school of thought.
- What is convincing about their arguments?
- What are the weak points in their arguments?
- Do those weak points really matter?
- Who were the main opponents of this approach?
- Names of key contributors and the decade (or year) when their contributions were made.
- Very brief details (a few lines at most) of the major pieces of research on this subject and why these are important.

Summarise

Summarise the essential information:

- as headings and key points, to structure the information;
- in several paragraphs, as the basis of an essay;
- in one paragraph, as a theme within an essay;
- in one sentence, in case you need to make only a brief reference to it, and for use in conclusions.

Active selection

Revising too much information can mean that you have to spend time in the exam deciding what not to include. It is more effective to work that out before the exam as part of the revision process. Give time not just to learning information, but to what you do not need to include for specific exam questions.

How much is 'enough'? (2)

Spot the difference

Two questions on the same subject could call for very different information. Don't aim to write everything you know on the subject: consider how the information you would include for each would differ, depending on the wording of the title.

Revising too few subjects

Before exams, it is common to hear students debating how few subjects or topics they can revise in order to pass the exam. Students can err by assuming that:

- There will be a question on each of the main topics they have revised. However, examiners may not set a question on some topics so, to be safe, you need to revise spare topics.
- Questions will be based on material covered in lectures and seminars. However, the questions set on your favourite topic may refer to material that required broader reading.
- Each question will be worded to cover only one topic. Often, questions are set to draw out your understanding of the links, similarities or contrasts between different parts of the course, calling on two or more topics.

Increase your chances of success

What is really 'key'?

Spend time identifying the information that is really key to answering specific questions that could be set for each revision topic: the main schools of thought, theories, research, debates, recent findings, and the significance of these – be very selective about any minor research and illustrative details.

Twice as many

Revise at least twice as many main topics as the number of questions you need to answer.

Multi-topic questions

Consider the obvious questions that could be set which would require you to compare, contrast or link material across the course. Prepare outline answers for such questions.

Breadth and currency

Read around the subject: don't just rely on your lecture notes. Show an interest in the broader debates of the subject. Be aware of how current research in your subject is developing into new areas and what issues are being raised by it.

Related sections

See: 'What are examiners looking for?' (p. 77).

See: 'Structured revision sessions' (p. 141).

Preparing a revision timetable

Avoid spending too much time planning revision and too little time actually revising. It is not unusual for people to waste time producing one revision timetable after another.

While it is useful to have a basic plan to ensure that you can cover the required number of topics, if you are spending revision time making more than quick adjustments to your timetable, consider:

- Are you writing out new revision timetables as a delaying tactic because you don't want to get down to study?
- Why is it that you are using such delaying tactics rather than actually revising? Do you need to take action to address these reasons?

A revision timetable does not need to be a work of art.

Plan your timetable

- **Use pencil** For paper-based timetables, plan in pencil and adapt your plan rather than writing a whole new plan.
- **Do it electronically** Use an electronic planner or create a table you can adapt easily.
- **Use your diary** Consider mapping out your revision goals into your diary or planner, so you are reminded of the next subjects and topics you will be revising whenever you look in the diary.
- **Use broad blocking** On your revision plan, identify broad subjects to look at over a longer time span, rather than planning out every hour.
- **Use variety** For long revision sessions, plan to include several themes or subjects, in order to maintain your attention.
- **Use starter activities** Plan activities for the start of each session, as this is a good way of focusing the mind.
- **Use alternation** Build in a balance of those topics you like with those you don't – avoid leaving everything you find difficult until last.
- **Use realism** You are more likely to follow your plan if it is manageable. Make sure you build in time to complete other essential tasks.

Make revision interesting (1)

Tick strategies that you could try for yourself.

Revise with others ☐ (p. 111)

Use colour! ☐

Use pencils, markers or other pens to highlight items in your notes, linking connected points by colour themes. Consider what character or tone the colours give to the topic.

People it ☐ (p. 122)

Use historical, fictional or sporting heroes to characterise material you are learning. Which combination of footballers, relatives or students would create that kind of chemical reaction? Which character would they be in the novel, play or legal case?

Vary the time ☐

Vary the amount of time you spend on each topic, so that within one longer session you have some short activities and some with a deeper focus. Spend several very short spells on topics you find difficult, rather than trying to absorb it all in one session.

Make revision interesting (2)

Invent likely questions ☐

Look up past exam questions on this or a similar subject. Invent similar questions of your own, based on the material you have covered. Thinking through likely questions helps to remember the material.

Chart it out ☐

Call upon your creative side to make the material look memorable and of visual interest.

Make a drawing that illustrates all the key points.

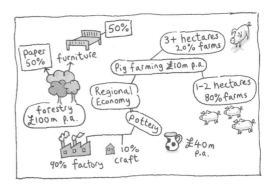

Find the links ☐

Look for connections between different parts of the subject. This may be of practical value in the exam if you are set questions that cut across several topics.

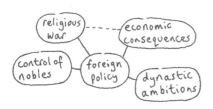

Read something new ☐

Browse new material if you feel you are growing stale, such as the last article written on the subject in a reputable journal.

Make revision interesting (3)

Take sides ☐

Don't just learn the different schools of thought – decide which you think is the more convincing and why.

This argument is by far the most convincing because, firstly, it…

Put it to music ☐

Sing or hum essential information to music. Link specific topics with different songs or tunes.

The hills are alive with the sound of the major theories in plate tectonics.

Change location ☐

fluorine chlorine etc

Excellent! I tubed that wave and I can recite the Periodic Table.

Use a different library. Go for a walk to refresh your mind. Revise by the river. Climb a hill.

Set personal challenges ☐

Complete 3 essay plans on reptiles by 5 p.m.

devise 3 mnemonics a day

write an essay plan in 3 minutes

Revising with others (1)

Revision doesn't have to be a solitary activity. Forming a study group can make revision much more interesting and effective.

Benefits of revising with others

Revising with others can be useful for:

- hearing different perspectives on the subject: other people will see topics differently from you so you gain a more rounded view of a topic;
- talking the subject through with others so you can clarify issues and pinpoint aspects that you need to investigate further;
- discussing and debating topics so that they are easier to recall in the exam;
- knowing that you are not alone in your revision, especially if you have been feeling isolated;
- mutual support to keep each other going, giving focus to each revision session and helping each other to use time effectively.

Forming an organised support group

If you prefer to study with other people, then either join a pre-existing study group or form one of your own. You can do this by:

- asking friends from your course to meet up to go over some difficult areas of your course together;
- advertising on a student noticeboard;
- advertising in a student newsletter;
- talking to your tutor, who may be able to put you in touch with other people who have said they want to study with others;
- speaking to student services at your college, or to support services in your student union; they may be able to help you set up a group.

Set ground rules

Mutually agreed ground rules help groups to bond, to remain focused and to settle disagreements more easily. Each group needs to decide which rules are right for it, but areas to discuss include:

- how often you will meet,
- when and where you will meet,
- how long sessions will last,
- whether you bring food or alcohol,
- how you will decide the membership. Does the group want to encourage new people to join, or to stop further membership if the group reaches a certain size?
- how you will decide what to revise in each session,
- how you want to spend your time revising together.

Revising with others (2)

How do you revise in a group?

Groups tend to be very individual and to develop their own ways of working. If you are unsure where to start, consider whether it is useful to:

- agree the purpose of each session in advance, so everyone can prepare for it;
- identify early on the topics that the group will cover, and which it won't, so individuals can plan their own revision around these;
- work on only one or two topics per session, looking at these from different angles;
- expect that everyone will prepare specific items for each session;
- put time aside for the social aspects at the end of the session, as a reward for time well spent.

Sharing out revision tasks

You can share out tasks for your exam preparation that save you all time, such as:

- hunting down information that everybody needs;
- finding past papers to work from;
- taking the lead on going over a topic;
- checking the latest journal articles for your subject;
- checking details about the exam itself;
- making arrangements for the group.

Avoid:

- spending time on sharing gloomy thoughts and building each other's negativity;
- supporting each other in wasting time;
- copying directly from each other's notes.

Things to do in revision groups

Check that your lecture notes are complete: other people may have understood lecture or seminar information differently. You may find you misheard or misunderstood an aspect of the subject.

Check whether you all share the same understanding of the subject: are there areas where you disagree?

Decide how to lay out the material for a complex topic in an easy-to-understand chart or diagram.

Debate the issues that are current for your subject.

Summarise key aspects of each major theory.

Summarise differences between the main schools of thought for your subject.

Go over past exam questions together: see how quickly you can identify the main points of each answer.

Where will it all go wrong?

Revision plans tend to start out as ambitious and well intentioned, but can be hard to maintain. Although we want our plans to work, it is wise to consider what might undermine them, so we can put measures into place to make sure they work.

Self-sabotage?

We are often our own worst enemies when it comes to revision. For example, we can:

- waste time – making endless cups of coffee, phoning friends, tidying where we rarely tidy, completing tasks that could wait until after the exam;
- work too hard, and become exhausted;
- keep postponing revision until a later date;
- revise late at night, making it hard to sleep, and hard to focus next day;
- allow friends to persuade us to do activities other than revision;
- plan poorly, so we run out of time to cover a reasonable number of topics;
- spend time worrying rather than just getting on with revision.

Other things that can go wrong

- Are friends or family likely to prevent us revising?
- Are there other aspects of our lives, such as children or work, that we need to plan around so our revision plans are realistic and practicable?

You CAN go to the ball, Cinderella! You can always revise after midnight!

Reflection

Are there ways you might sabotage your own revision strategy? How will you take steps to prevent these from sabotaging your revision?

What other things might hinder your revision? How will you manage these so they don't hold you back?

Closing comments

Summary Key points

★ Start early – give yourself the time you need.

★ Select revision topics carefully.

★ Devise a strategy: don't just reread your notes.

★ Make it enjoyable – it will be as stimulating or boring as you make it.

★ Mix it up for interest – use varied approaches.

★ Revise with the right people – for different perspectives and motivation.

Revision is an essential part of your exam preparation. There isn't one way to revise, and ultimately you must decide the combination of strategies and techniques that works for you, based on experimentation and the results you achieve. The test of what works is partly the marks that you attain, as gaining good results is likely to be your prime purpose. However, consider too your level of interest, enjoyment and engagement during revision sessions, and the long-term knowledge and understanding of your subject that your revision gives you.

Part of good exam preparation is working out what could get in the way of you revising what you need, and making sure you have plans to manage such distractions and difficulties. Other people may well present you with good reasons for why you should revise differently. This may be because such methods worked for them, or because they have their own motives for distracting you. However, you must identify the approaches that work best for you. Avoid revising in a particular way simply because other people do.

Good revision strategies are likely to lead to at least a reasonable exam pass, and probably much better. However, if you want to gain really good marks, then a broader preparation is recommended than simply focusing on revision. Such a broad approach includes developing strategies to manage your emotions and levels of stress, and understanding the links between these and your performance levels in the exam.

Chapter 8

Memory: Remembering what we want, when we need it

Learning outcomes

This chapter supports you in:

- understanding your memory so you can use it more effectively
- managing memory anxiety
- identifying what you need to remember for exams
- training your memory to improve recall
- devising mnemonics to recall details
- building knowledge architectures to support your memory efficiency

Remembering what you have learnt so that you can use material flexibly and at speed is an important aspect of most types of exam. Students often worry about the effectiveness of their memory for exam performance. However, we can train the memory to deal with the demands made of it under exam conditions. Knowing more about how memory works makes it easier to identify techniques that will help you to recall what you want when you need to.

In exams, you do not need to be able to repeat course information by rote. Indeed, relying on that kind of memory ability can be a disadvantage. In exams, you need to be able to use material flexibly, rather than be constrained by having learnt it in a particular order. You benefit more from developing knowledge structures that make your subject meaningful to you, and considering what you really need to remember in order to answer particular questions.

Your capacity for recalling information under exam conditions is helped through working with your material, organising it, reducing it down, and applying it. Practice in answering exam questions reinforces recall. Specific techniques in training the memory gives you added control over information once in the exam.

About memory

Making memory work for us

If you feel concerned about remembering material in the exam, be reassured that you can train your memory to work more effectively. However, it can take time to identify which techniques work best for you and to practise these.

In an exam, we rely on the 'recall' aspect of memory. However, our ability to recall under exam conditions depends on how effective we are at encoding information into memory in the first place. The effort we take to make information memorable is usually more relevant to our remembering it than whether we were born with 'good memories' or not. Our memories usually reward us for the time, effort and imagination we put into building good mental structures of the information we want to recall.

Memory work takes time

People who are very successful at exams generally leave little to chance. They revise intensely, building knowledge architectures over the longer term, and making use of many different memory strategies in the lead-up to an exam. This means they have much greater control over what they can remember at a given time. Memory is not a mental facility separate from other aspects of study and life, as the following considerations indicate.

Over-efficiency

Paradoxically, one reason we don't remember things is because of the brain's efficiency. When it sees items that are familiar and unthreatening, the brain tends to register them as uninteresting and unimportant. There is no need to pay them attention or to remember them. If we want to be sure to remember things, we need to make the brain:

- stop and take note of what is before it,
- understand what it is taking in,
- pay attention and take in details,
- use techniques to aid recall: e.g. register something novel or 'memorable' about it.

About memory: Nurturing the memory

Memory doesn't function in a vacuum. Our brain needs the right chemicals and rest in order to function at its peak.

Eating for exams

You probably have a good sense of what constitutes 'sensible eating' and a 'balanced diet', even if you do not follow this at all times. However, for peak exam performance, it is worth eating a reasonably balanced diet for several weeks or months before the exam (p. 200). Eating food that makes you feel comfortable and content is better than feeling you are punishing yourself, so give thought to how you can make your food appetising.

Brain food

Research into food that stimulates cognitive effectiveness is still relatively new. However, some foods seem to boost performance (Holford, 2002).

Omega-3 and omega-6

Children who received these omega supplements for 3 months showed improved rates of concentration and reading skills, compared with the control group who didn't receive these oils (Richardson and Montgomery, 2005). Omega-3 and omega-6 can be found in oily fish such as mackerel and in flax oil.

Isoflavins

Isoflavins are natural plant oestrogens found in soya foods. These appear to improve memory function. Students who were placed on a high-soya diet showed significant improvements in different memory functions, including long-term recall. They also showed improved mental flexibility, being able to manipulate information better (File et al., 2001).

Liquids

Water helps electromagnetic activity in the brain. The effect is not the same when sugar, milk, caffeine or other chemicals are added. Even mild dehydration, at levels of 2% dehydration and above, can have a significant effect on memory and cognitive functioning (Sharma et al., 1986).

Warburton et al. (2001) found that commercially available energy drinks that contain caffeine and taurine led to better information processing than either sugar-free or sugar-rich drinks. However, excess coffee drinking can impair academic performance and induce feelings of stress and anxiety.

About memory: Unconscious working

Sleep

We remember better if we:

- revise material, then
- sleep, then
- review it the next day.

Ahh! Now I understand. The offside rule will elude me no more!

While we sleep, the brain absorbs what we have learnt

While we are in deep, slow-wave sleep, the part of the brain known as the cortex goes to work in making sense of what we learnt and experienced in the day, assimilating new material. If we don't have such deep sleep between when we revise and when we sit the exam, we lose this unconscious cortical advantage.

Time and the unconscious

Even when we are awake our unconscious mind works on the material we have covered so far. We can notice this when we have been struggling to understand a particular area, and then suddenly it makes sense. For some people, it can take weeks or months for the brain to make sense of material. This is why relying exclusively on working just before the exam can be a disadvantage.

It is less likely we will remember new material learnt only on the day of the exam, as the waking and sleeping brain won't have had a chance to act upon the material.

The power of rest breaks

The unconscious mind carries on working even when we are not studying, so taking breaks is not a disadvantage. Frequent breaks can help the brain to absorb new information. Going for a walk, for example, can both work off excess nervous energy, and refresh your thinking.

Mull it over

It is important to give your mind time to mull over information, both through active reflection and by the unconscious connections it makes over time. This helps secure material in memory as part of your longer-term knowledge architectures.

Managing memory anxiety

Anxiety about memory

It is not at all unusual for students to worry about their memory.

I know I won't remember a thing once I am in the exam

I've always had a very bad memory.

I won't do well in the exams: other people have better memories than me.

Managing the anxiety

If you worry about your memory, then there are steps you can take.

1 Find mental calm

Remember that stress and anxiety, in themselves, can make it hard to remember. Therefore, your first consideration is managing stress. You can help your memory to function better if you learn to move quickly to a state of mental calm. See Chapter 10.

2 Give your memory credit

People generally under-estimate their memories. If you start to worry about your memory capacity, focus on everything it does remember, not the individual occasions when it forgets.

3 Don't over-estimate other people's memories

Although there are apparent differences in people's memories, these can usually be accounted for by reasons such as plentiful exposure to the material to be remembered, which helps build good knowledge architectures, and by their confidence and practice in using memory strategies. Very few students have good exam memories if they haven't used such approaches.

4 Memory can be trained

Your current level of memory performance isn't a constant for all time. There are techniques and strategies that you can use to improve the way you remember things.

About memory: Layered approaches

Coaching not forcing

The memory doesn't respond well to being forced. If it isn't delivering what you need, move on to something else, and come back to it later. Often, the information you need will come to mind once you stop searching for it.

Layered memories

Our understanding of new material and our recall of it can be built up in layers. This is especially useful for difficult and complex material. First, look for the easiest and simplest text or version. Use this to provide a basic foundation before moving on to more difficult material.

The first time you cover the information, you may only get a vague sense of the topic. The second

time, you will start to recognise some of the information as familiar. By the third time, you are likely to be looking actively for what is familiar, as well as noticing variations. You should start to look consciously for details such as names and dates, and see if you can remember them without looking.

Each time you cover the material from a different angle, your brain will build up a richer memory impression of the material, making it easier to recall in the future.

Working in this way means that, even if you are anxious in an exam and can't remember some fine details from the higher layers, such as layer 5 on the diagram below, you are more likely to remember the foundation information (layers 1–3). Once you start using these, they may prompt the memory for details from higher layers.

---

5 Specialist and wider reading; more focused approach to remembering specific details.

---

4 Reading around the subject to understand issues, unusual applications, controversies, related material.

---

3 A more thorough approach to understanding the core information and some unusual features.

---

2 Less basic, more detailed reading.

---

1 Rough outline and basic facts.

About memory: 'More than once'

Compound experience

We build up a more exact memory if we are exposed to the same material from several different perspectives. This builds an elaborate internal 'picture', or 'schema', of what we are trying to recall. We are more likely to build sophisticated mental schema if we combine information taken from different points of view and varied sources (books, journals, direct experience, reflection, our own notes, discussion) than simply by going over the same material from one book or our notes.

Whose style suits?

Sometimes it is difficult to make sense of information when we read or hear about it from only one source. It may seem that reading about the subject in other sources will make us even more confused. However, each author will write about a subject in slightly different ways, with individual emphases, alternative references or their own explanations. Reading several accounts means that we are more likely to find a version that fits the way we take in information: we are more likely to find the account that makes sense to us.

Repetition counts

The more times we encounter something, the more we are likely to recall it. When revising, covering similar ground several times for shorter periods is more likely to be effective than spending a long time on the same material on only one occasion.

Repetition helps you remember information a long time into the future.

Repetition helps you remember information a long time into the future.

Repetition helps you remember information a long time into the future.

About memory: Special effects

'Startle effect'

If something stands out as odd, bizarre or unexpected in any way, the surprise of this can help to log the information in the memory. You can create a 'startle effect' by simple devices such as the way you lay information out on the page, use of colour to help you remember a page of information, or applying the material to an unexpected context.

For example, to remember blood vessels, imagine them running down the outside of your body with labels on flagpoles bearing their names. The more unusual, strange or shocking, the stronger the impression on your memory.

'People effect'

Even as babies, humans tend to find faces more absorbing than any other information. Information associated with real people can be more memorable. You can create this effect by linking people and characters relevant to you with the material you have to learn.

For example, imagine your favourite musicians, pop idols, TV characters, football players or historic heroes explaining your subject: hear the details in their voices. Imagine them as the focus of research findings: how would these results imact upon their lives? Or how would they respond if they heard these research results in a press conference or if they were the client whose personal or business problems you are solving?

Newton says 'For every action, there must be an equal and opposite reaction.'

Exam memory

The role of memory in exams

Because many students worry about remembering information in exams, educators often downplay the role of memory. Instead, they emphasise other important factors, such as understanding the material and working steadily over time. These aspects are extremely important. However, it remains true that memory plays an important role in exam performance.

Although exams are not just about memory:

- it clearly helps if we can remember the material we have covered;
- we are likely to feel more confident in exams if we feel we can recall the material we need.

'Exam memory'

Exam memory is different from most kinds of everyday memory. In order to function in our daily lives, we call constantly on our memories. We remember most of what we need to remember with little apparent effort. Exam memory is different because it requires recall of particular information in a specific moment. People who work steadily over the course of their programme can build solid knowledge architectures (see p. 136). As a result, recalling material in exams may seem as easy to them as remembering everyday information.

However, if we want to be more certain of recalling what we want when we need it, we can benefit from employing specific additional strategies that aid recall. This gives increased control over our memory and the material.

Exam memory isn't 'card trick' memory

Exam memory does not require mastery of 'party-trick' skills, such as remembering the order of long lists of numbers or playing cards seen only once. You can develop good recall for course material without such 'super skills' – and most students do well without these.

What will I need to remember?

What do I need to remember for essay-based exams?

Exam essays are shorter than those produced as coursework. You need to remember:

- material for at least twice the number of topics as the number of questions you are required to answer, in order to have a reasonable choice of questions;
- the key points for each specific question, listed as headings, with details organised in level of importance beneath those headings;
- less detail about each key point than you would need for a coursework essay;
- the key names and dates to cite to support each point you might wish to make;
- background information that helps you make sense of the subject in your own mind, but only very brief background details for inclusion in your exam answers.

Remember:

- You probably won't have time to include more minor references and details so don't worry if you haven't time to learn these.
- You need to select from, and organise, your material differently to answer specific questions on the same topic (see Chapter 9).

What do I need to remember for short-answer and multiple-choice exams?

- It is difficult to avoid learning all aspects of your programme for short-answer exams and multiple choice questions.
- You need to know the key points and references, organised under headings or questions, for all aspects of your programme.
- Consider, as you revise, whether information you are learning lends itself to being tested as a multiple-choice or short-answer question. If so, jot that information down onto a card, and carry the cards around with you to test your recall in spare moments.

Technical subjects

You will need to learn:

- Typical problems and the theories and procedures to apply to solve them.
- Each step in the problem-solving procedures, in the correct order.
- Very precise information, exactly as it was given to you, as well as a general understanding of the concepts.
- Mathematical formulae.

Train the brain: Grouping and labelling

Around 5 things

It is easier to remember information if you break it into around five groups or 'chunks'. It is harder to remember 6 or more chunks. If this still leaves you with many 'chunks' to remember, group these further, until you have several layers of 3–5 chunks:

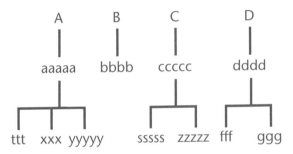

Labels matter

Giving a descriptive name to each group helps you remember it.

Like with like

Group similar material together: it will feel as though there is less to remember, and will reinforce your recall of related information.

More can be easier than less

It isn't how much we have to remember that really matters, but how well we organise this information in the memory. It can be easier to remember *more* information than remembering *less*, if it is well organised. For example, it can be easier to learn 10 items than 7, if you:

● break the 10 items into 3 sets of 3–4 items, AND
● find an association between the 3 items;
● actively consider a way of recalling the information later.

> **Example: List of 10**
> Time yourself learning this list of items.
> (1) oranges   (2) bridge   (3) arteries   (4) sun
> (5) chocolate   (6) veins   (7) limes   (8) horse
> (9) capillaries   (10) lemons

Logical groups or categories

It is worth looking first for logical groups. Six of the items belong to 2 categories, blood vessels and citrus fruit. Labelling these makes it easier to remember those 6 items, even though the total amount of material to remember, including the labels, is then greater.

> **Example**
> Blood vessels: arteries, veins, capillaries
> Citrus fruit: oranges, lemons, limes

Train the brain: The power of association

The basis of almost all memory training is exploiting the power of association. Memory works by making links between new material that we encounter in our daily lives and what the brain has already learnt, including very familiar information such as colours, music, relatives, childhood experiences, TV programmes.

Creative association

The final four items from the list on p. 125 are not logically linked. These are easier to remember if you make a creative association. For example:

- **tall tale** Imagine the 4 items in a scene or story that immediately links them.
- **picture** Visualise the 4 items in an unusual association.

Whichever method you use, it is important to find the version that captures your own imagination. Each of the following scenarios would be easier for individual people to recall:

- the sun melting a horse made of chocolate, which pours away under a bridge;
- a chocolate-coloured horse watches the sun rise over a bridge;
- riding a horse over a bridge at sunset and feeding it a piece of chocolate.

'bit hot'

Using association for course material

Most of the material you need to remember for exams will be logically linked, but the logic may not be immediately apparent to your brain. This may be because you don't know the material well enough yet to know the link (for example, you might not have known that capillaries were blood vessels). Names and technical terms or words in other languages can also lack an immediately logical link. You can use different kinds of associations to remember programme material. These associations can include:

- personal meaning,
- a sense of place,
- organisational devices,
- your senses, to provide visual and sound cues.

Train the brain: Make material meaningful

It must 'make sense'

If the material doesn't make sense to you, it will be much harder to remember it.

1   Check initial understanding

Check whether you understand the material as you read through. Does it seem to make sense? If not, stop and work out what is meant.

2   Write it out

Jot down an outline of the material without checking your notes. If you need to keep checking, this may indicate you haven't fully understood it.

3   Apply it

Can you recall the material easily, in your own words, when answering past exam papers, or questions you set yourself?

4   Explain it to someone else

Can you explain the material to someone else without feeling that you, or they, are becoming confused? Encourage them to ask you questions, and see whether you can answer these.

Make meaning

If the material doesn't make much sense to you:

- Go over it again, to get the gist.
- Reread it, focusing on difficult areas.
- Discuss it with someone who knows the subject.
- Read different publications. These may explain or present the material in alternative ways that suit you better.
- Write out the material in your own words.
- Draw a chart or diagram to connect the different aspects.

Personal connections

It is easier to remember information when it is linked to material that has special personal significance. You could link course material to:

- significant numbers in your own life, such as birthdays or house numbers;
- people you know or have read about or seen on TV;
- how you and people you know could be affected by an issue, or how they would respond in a given situation.

Train the brain: Organise the information

Organisation

The brain finds it much easier to remember well-organised information.

1. It can find information more quickly and easily if you organise it logically.
2. It organises information in its own way if you don't help it to organise it in the way you really want to recall it.
3. When you organise course material, you are working with it in an interactive way, which helps you to remember it in the future.

Break it into sections

It is easier to remember material if it is sub-divided into key areas. You can then recall how many sections there are, either as a number, or as a visual memory of blocks of material. This also makes it easier to select and manipulate the material to meet the requirements of specific questions.

Label it

Give each section a short, clear label that sums up what the section is about, much like the headings used on this page. This could be written as a question followed by the answer.

Number it

It is easier to remember a list if you know how many items there are on it, so:

- Number your items.
- Mentally state the numbers when you go over the list.
- Test yourself: how many items are on the list? Which item is associated with which number?

List it

Lists are the easiest structure to draw up, to carry round and check in spare moments.

```
4 types of snake
1 viper
2 cobra
3 asp
4 very scary
```

Structure it

It is easier to recall information if it is structured well. This means:

- identifying the most significant points;
- ordering points in order of importance;
- breaking each key area down into sections;
- identifying the sub-points for each section;
- organising all of this into a diagram, chart or physical shape. This makes it is easier to see how one piece of information relates to all the rest.

Train the brain: Use your senses (1)

Sense sensitivity

Memory is 'sense sensitive'. It can work more efficiently and effectively depending on:

- how many of our senses, sight, sound, touch, we use when we are learning the material (other senses are less effective for exam purposes as we can't reproduce the same conditions to recall the information once in the exam room);
- whether we have included our preferred sense or senses when learning the material: we tend to have personal preferences for one or more senses, and it helps to use these when learning material;
- active use of those senses, especially our preferred sense, when we are trying to recall the material in the exam.

Visual memory

You may have a sense of where on the page, or in your notes, material was recorded, which, in turn, helps prompt the mind to remember it in full. If you can 'see' where something is on the page when you try to recall it, this suggests a good visual memory. If so, developing your visual memory further may help you gain control of your memory for course material.

Build visual memory

Assist your visual memory by:

- giving your brain additional opportunities to 'see' information, drawing attention to visual characteristics;
- presenting your material in visually distinct ways, such as diagrams, charts, pictures and cartoons;
- making each page look different by the way you lay out the information and use shape and colour;
- checking actively to see where information appears on the page;
- moving your eyes across surfaces in an organised way, from leading points to less important ones, so that your 'motor' memory reinforces the visual memory;.
- using colour and shape to highlight themes throughout a book, or to show where information can be found in a diagram or on the page.

Train the brain: Use your senses (2)

Tactile and motor memory

You may find it easier to remember material through practical activities, 'doing' and 'feeling'. This is referred to as kinaesthetic memory. For example, the act of making a diagram, or writing out information, may be what helps you to remember material, rather than 'seeing' it. You may remember a piece of music through playing it or clicking your fingers to it, rather than reading music or hearing it in your mind. If this sounds like you, the following strategies may work best for you.

Text yourself

If you find something hard to remember, write it as a text message to yourself.

Write it out

You may find that writing or typing material out several times helps you to recall it.

Track it

Use your fingers to track information down columns, or to link information on a diagram.

Sub-vocalise it

Speaking the material under your breath without sounding out the words aloud can help your body to remember the information, as this still requires fine muscle movements, and you can do this subtly in the exam to recall the information.

Auditory memory

If you find it easier to remember information by going over it verbally, recalling where you heard it, or by repeating information verbally, then you are likely to have a preference for learning through auditory methods. If so, the following strategies may be particularly useful for you.

Learn it to music

- Revise each topic to specific music
- Rap it, hum it, or sing it
- Chant the material to a strong beat

Listen in

- Download material to listen to on your MP3 player
- Take part in discussions and debates

Use your voice

- Say it aloud
- Read it aloud, record it, and play it back

Train the brain: Locus method

Locus is the Latin word for 'place' or 'location'. This is an ancient way of recalling material. Scholars associated information with particular places. The layout of a location, such as a series of columns, pathways, plants or windows, can provide a pre-made structure for organising material.

Many people still use this method today. It is relatively easy to use and it is practical. You can call upon scenes that are familiar to you, or simply attach sheets bearing the material around your home, onto chairs, windows and stairwells.

Consider which buildings, rooms and outdoor locations you can assign to each topic. Decide whether you would prefer to:

● walk around the location to recall the material;
● attach material physically around your home;
● visualise the material in association with a place;
● draw a map to help you remember what material is associated with which location;
● narrate which information is located where.

Auditory memory and the locus method

Rehearse, verbally, which information you associate with which room. Recite this as a verbal list, or narrate a journey from room to room.

Kinaesthetic memory and the locus method

Walk around the location, making physical contact with the information: point, touch it, trace the information. Mentally retrace your route. If you can 're-walk' the journey, mentally, in the exam, this can help bring the information to mind.

Visual memory and the locus method

Make a visual journey through the location, seeing the material attached to furniture and other items, to bring the information to mind.

Personal mnemonics

What is a 'mnemonic'?

Mnemonics are devices that help us to remember more easily. They work by associating information that is new or more difficult to recall with other material that is easier for us to remember. However, what works for one person won't necessarily do so for anyone else. We need to experiment to find the associations that work for us and the material.

What works as a mnemonic?

Anything might work for us, as memory is very individual. However, as we saw on p.122, some types of association are more likely to work than others. Useful starting places for devising new mnemonics are:

● bizarre, strange and silly associations;
● rhymes, songs and raps;
● strong visual images;
● striking or well-known locations;
● rude or shocking associations;
● odd but memorable combinations;
● links to already-known ordered sets of information, such as numbers, playing cards and colours of the rainbow.

Most of us will be familiar, from school, with ways of remembering the colours of the rainbow in the right order: red, orange, yellow, green, blue, indigo, violet.

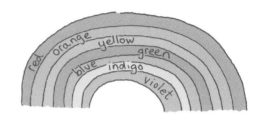

First-letter invented words

Many people were taught to remember the colours of the rainbow by remembering an invented word that comprises the sounds of the first letters of all seven colours: ROYGBIV.

First-letter rhymes

Other people remember rainbow colours by associating the first letter of each colour with a different word of a simple rhyme:

Richard Of York Gave Battle In Vain.

Narratives to aid recall

The 'story' below relates to the bile pigment bilirubin, which is yellow in colour. Bilirubin has been cited as an antioxidant, which protects cells against the effects of free radicals in the body.

Billy Rubin always wore a yellow T-shirt. He worked at the local prison where he protected the cells from attacks by a local gang, 'The Free Radicals'.

Mnemonics: facts and figures

Dates and numbers

Dates and numbers can be the hardest to remember as they are very specific. To recall these, you can:

- repeat them to a beat;
- break them down into smaller numbers;
- link them to personal numbers, such as family birthdays, house numbers, months of the year, or signs of the zodiac;
- give each number a colour;
- associate each number with an object that looks like it, such as a swan for number 2, and build up a visual picture of the items;
- associate each number with an object that sounds like it, such as 2 with 'gnu', and 4 with 'door', and devise a 'sound' sequence or story to help you recall the numbers: 'gnu at the door, 24'.

Definitions and formulae

These are usually learnt best through repetition and practical use. Recite them as a rap or sing them, visualise them, apply them several times, write them out until you can do so without looking.

Fact-and-figure stories

If you need to remember many disparate pieces of information, link these together into one longer narrative or 'story'. The story doesn't need to make sense – nonsense or fabulous tales may be more memorable. Fill the story with events that lead you to the information you need, in the order you are likely to use it. Visualise the characters and scene and give it atmosphere to help you remember it.

Example: Fabulous tale

- Her name is (lead researcher for article).
- She stands in a clearing in a dark and icy wood about which little is known, located at X (e.g. place after which a school of thought is named).
- She was born in: (date of key research)
- Three bolts of thunder explode into the sky, each associated with one aspect of the research. The second bolt is the loudest as that was the most significant.
- Her arch enemy, the evil duke X, appears in a cloud of red dust – he has arrived from the X desert (where an opposing theory was developed).
- He carries daggers (two aspects of the theory), etc.

Recall v. knowledge

Speedy recall in exams

The methods described above for improving exam recall can be built up over time, but are more usually employed during the last few weeks of revision. The strategies that are described for recalling information are useful for being able to work at speed in:

- recalling information;
- seeing quickly how that information links to other material;
- being able to select the most relevant information easily;
- planning answers based on key information;
- recalling details.

Limits of information-based approaches

The memory approaches described so far are largely information-based. Such approaches to revision have advantages for speedy and organised recall. However, they can mean that other aspects, such as relative significance and subject understanding, are neglected. Without a good understanding of the subject, it can be harder to manipulate information to answer unexpected questions or to make good choices about what to include and what to leave out. This can result in exam answers that:

- are cluttered with unnecessary detail;
- have too little focus and direction, so the examiner can't see your point of view or argument;
- make insufficient analysis of the material;
- demonstrate a weak understanding of what the question is looking for.

Knowledge and mental versatility

Students who do well in exams tend to know the subject very well. This is not simply about memory. Indeed, some students can produce good answers by drawing only on the depth of their background knowledge, and the information they have absorbed over time, rather than by using any specific memory strategies.

Such knowledge provides mental versatility, so that the student can answer a broad range of questions with confidence: they 'know the subject in their bones', so memory strategies aren't so critical to them. A student who can combine good knowledge architectures with good memory strategies can feel very confident about exams.

© Stella Cottrell (2006, 2012) *The Exam Skills Handbook*, Palgrave Macmillan

From information to exam knowledge

Information we have gathered about a subject becomes really useful when it ceases being external data, and becomes part of our internal knowledge systems. This can take place in a number of ways. For the purpose of exams, this usually means working with the material in the ways outlined below.

Focusing

Identifying the specific topics, themes and exam questions that we need to know about.

Gathering

Bringing together the relevant information from our notes, lectures, books, and other sources into one set of notes.

Sifting

Selecting relevant material to work with further, and putting other material aside.

Reducing

Condensing remaining material down to the essentials, so that we retain only material we have a realistic chance of using in the exam.

Organising

Setting out material in ways that help us to find it, use it, recall it quickly and apply it easily. Students often do this by putting material into numbered lists, index cards, clear and well-organised charts, colourful diagrams, etc.

Hunting

Identifying any remaining gaps in our information and hunting these down.

Manipulating

Working with the information in detail, considering which is most relevant to particular questions. In the exam, we need to be able to select and apply material flexibly, depending on the specific question that is set.

Tips

- Work quickly – set yourself time limits.
- Work on several related exam questions at once, considering the differences between them.
- Set yourself limits for the number of cards or pages you will use for each theme: you are then more likely to cut out material you don't need.
- Write information out in your own words to help visual, auditory and motor memory.
- Write out information step by step to draw your attention to each stage in a process.

Building knowledge architectures: Want to know

What are knowledge architectures?

A knowledge architecture can be considered as a more elaborate set of connections within the brain. When people work on a particular area over time, they develop many neural links in the brain, so that that aspect of the brain becomes more developed. A strong knowledge architecture is likely to include understanding not just of the core subject, but also of its unusual or atypical aspects, and its connections to related topics.

The benefit of elaborated knowledge architectures

Those who know a subject well can tend to take in new information about that subject more quickly: they can see easily where it 'fits in'. In other words, their existing knowledge helps their assimilation of new material. For example, if they know that there has been a lack of research evidence to support a particular theory, and a new research paper provides that evidence, they may be able to recognise, instantly, why that paper is significant to the subject and why it is worth mentioning.

When we know less about a subject, it can take us much longer to make sense of new material, recognise relevance, and make good judgements about its significance. We can feel we are

stupid for not grasping the subject quickly and remembering it, when really we just don't yet know enough about it.

How can we build good knowledge architectures?

Knowledge structures are normally developed over time: they are not usually a feature of 'last-minute revision'. We build knowledge structures through measures such as:

- continued exposure;
- interacting with material;
- questioning and reflecting.

Wanting to know

There is no real substitute for genuine interest in the subject. This makes it a pleasure to spend time finding out more, which means that you are likely to spend more time reading around the subject and actively thinking about it. Such activity tends to raise questions to which you want answers, motivating you to further investigation.

As this quest for knowledge is motivated by interest, the information is associated with excitement rather than anxiety. If you can reproduce that excited interest during the exam, this aids recall. It also contributes to the sense of 'flow' and ease associated with peak performance.

Building knowledge architectures: Gain the overview

Read around the subject

It is expected that students in higher education will spend a good deal of their time reading around the subject. This means reading the set texts, but also looking beyond these to other material that you choose to read to pursue particular areas of interest.

Gain a bird's eye view

Aim to build up a good overview of the subject, so that you feel 'on top of the subject'. This will help you answer a broader range of questions, and to see how details and new material fit into the bigger picture. For example, ask yourself:

- How did your subject develop? Who raised which questions?
- What have been the key pieces of research?
- What are the major controversies in the subject? Why do these differences in opinion exist?
- What is new in the subject?
- How do the different aspects of the subject link together?

What if the subject doesn't interest me?

If you are not particularly interested in the subject, this is likely to be a disadvantage. You can work around this as follows:

- Look, actively, for a point of interest; the more we know about a subject, the easier it is to generate such interest.
- Set specific questions to guide your search for answers.
- Find a personal connection to the subject. For example, where might this material become relevant to a situation you can find yourself in? This could be anything, from a time when this knowledge could save your life, to making better connections with a friend or relative who has an interest in a related topic.

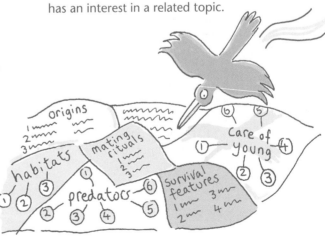

Building knowledge architectures: Interact

If there is one change that most students could make to improve their revision strategies, it would be to engage more interactively with the material. All too often, students report that they spend long hours reading through their notes, getting bored with the material. Whether for revision or for coursework, you are likely to benefit if you look for ways of making the subject more your own.

Search for significance

Students who struggle with exams, or even with coursework, tend to complain that they don't know what examiners are looking for, or that they aren't sure what to include and what to leave out. This suggests difficulties in being able to recognise what is really significant to the subject.

Recognition of significance can come simply through knowing about the subject. You can help to develop your appreciation of significance by working actively with material:

- Find out more about the subject so you can see how the pieces fit together.
- Identify those questions that remain to be answered through further research in the subject: these are sometimes described in the later sections of research articles.

- Identify areas of controversy within the subject – so that you can see where new material adds to, or contradicts, existing debate.
- Consider what would be needed to reconcile the differences that exist in areas of controversy, or between the major schools of thought within the subject.

Answer your own questions

One way of interacting with the material is to identify questions that you want answered and then set about answering them. Many students are good at generating the questions – indeed, some poorer essays are little more than a series of questions. Asking questions can be a way of deflecting attention from your not knowing the answers. Once you set your question, hunt out answers.

Even if you find it hard to find answers to some of your questions, it is likely that, during your search, you will encounter a range of material that provides interest, context, background knowledge, and a better overall sense of the subject. At some point, you will recall this, unexpectedly, just when you need it.

Building knowledge architectures: Chart the detail

People vary in whether they prefer to gain an overview first, and then add the detail to this, or whether they prefer to build from the details towards the big picture. Either way, it is important to keep referring backwards and forwards between the big picture and the detail, in order to:

- develop a sense of how everything fits together;
- make links easily within the subject;
- build a good understanding of the subject.

Charting

Produce a chart that clarifies:

- the key schools of thought for different topics;
- the names and research associated with these;
- how these approaches build on each other's findings;
- how they are similar to each other;
- where they contrast with each other;
- the strengths and weaknesses of each approach under different circumstances.

Example   Chart outline: Tracking developments in an area of research

Date of publication	Name(s) associated with the research	Key findings	Significance and impact of findings	Other comments/ details

You can find a copy of this for photocopying in Appendix 6 (p. 272).

Closing comments

Summary Key points

★ Experiment – so you get to know the strengths of your own memory.

★ Help your memory through the right sleep and nutrition.

★ Build up layers of memory by returning to material in different ways over time.

★ Organise your material into manageable blocks.

★ Select carefully – what do you really need to recall?

★ Re-present your material to yourself in ways that spark the memory.

★ Train your brain, working with its natural ways of functioning.

★ Know your subject inside out – knowledge helps recall.

★ Balance detail with broader overview.

Our memories are remarkable – and much more powerful than we often imagine. We rarely notice how much we rely on them to make sense of each aspect of our daily experience. Although memory is complex, we know enough about it to train our minds to be more effective at recalling what we need for exams.

Successful students tend to be systematic in going over material from a number of angles, on several occasions, over a period of time. They build their understanding and memory in layers, so they feel more secure about their exam recall. This can, in turn, build their confidence, which in turn makes them feel calmer so they are more likely to think clearly and recall what they need.

The most successful students take care to provide their memory with every opportunity to function well. They rest, they eat well, they give the memory 'down time' to process information and make sense of it.

From an intellectual perspective, the best students tend to be those who take the time to build knowledge architectures. These provide strong memory structures to help them remember how information fits together, what is significant and why. In an exam, such students can not only recall facts and figures, but can manipulate material flexibly, easily and at speed, as appropriate to the questions they have selected. They know how their subject material is perceived from different perspectives and schools of thought and can draw conclusions for questions they have not yet encountered.

You can develop these skills through practice, such as through the structured revision sessions recommended in Chapter 9, and by using the memory techniques outlined in this chapter.

Chapter 9

Structured revision sessions

Learning outcomes

This chapter supports you in:

- recognising the importance of planning your revision sessions
- identifying practical revision activities
- improving your information management to support revision
- planning individual revision sessions
- developing a revision strategy that builds on previous revision sessions
- using practice questions and mock exams effectively

One of the most common difficulties that students have with revision is knowing quite what they are supposed to do. They wonder where to start, what other students are doing, and whether they could be doing something more useful to prepare for their exams.

This chapter offers a series of structured sessions to help you manage revision time effectively, organise your material to make revision easier, and plan your revision strategy. If you are uncertain where to begin your revision, then these sessions provide a starting point.

Students can be reluctant to undertake practice papers or mock exams because they consider the experience too far removed from real exam conditions. Although it is true that your adrenalin, motivation and ability to focus may be different in the exam room, pre-exam practice is nevertheless invaluable. You identify what you really know and how you perform. You develop your ability to work at speed. It is likely that the questions you practise in advance will help with those you ultimately select in the exam. This chapter provides guidance on how to use practice sessions to improve your exam performance.

Why bother planning revision sessions?

Introduction

It is not unusual for students to plan out a revision timetable days, weeks or months ahead of the exam, and even to spend time making this look good, reviewing it, and rewriting it, focusing on the topics they will cover.

Despite this, they tend to be reluctant to devote any time at all to planning individual revision sessions and thinking through the strategies they will apply in these. This can be a mistake, as planning out revision sessions:

● provides a natural starting point;
● helps focus the mind quickly right from the beginning of a session;
● avoids wasting time in sessions through distractions and daydreaming;
● ensures the session is of real value.

Without such planning, it is easy to fall into a dull, predictable, unproductive routine:

● reading through notes in an unfocused way;
● doing the same things every session, and becoming bored;
● daydreaming and finding excuses for doing something else.

The 'time paradox'

Even if you are used to exam revision, it can be rather daunting to know there are hours of unstructured revision time ahead, all devoted to one large subject. It can feel, simultaneously, as though there is not enough time to cover everything and also that there is too much time until the exam. Until the last minute, it can seem as though there is too much time left to provide the necessary sense of urgency, but not enough time to learn everything.

This apparent contradiction can make it difficult to settle down to revision. However, planning individual sessions can help you to manage the time paradox, by providing short-term goals and outcomes.

Session outlines

As it can be difficult to start planning individual sessions, several outline structures are provided here to help you begin the process. You can use these as suggested, or adapt them to suit your own requirements. There is no set length for a session, and you may find it easier to break one session into several shorter ones, or to continue, after a short break, into successive sessions, building on one topic.

Revision session 1: Familiarity with the exam paper

About this session

The aim of this session is to develop your knowledge of what you can reasonably expect in your exam.

Motivation

Knowing what is expected will make it easier to plan out future sessions effectively. The more familiar you are with the questions, the easier it is to spot the information you need when you go through your notes. Furthermore, the more familiar you are with the way questions are set, the more likely it is that you will feel the questions in your exam are 'old friends', and there is less likelihood of unpleasant surprises in the exam room.

Focus

The focus of the session is developing an understanding of what to expect from exam papers, based on previous exam papers for your subject. The exam paper should then feel familiar to you once you enter the exam room, making you feel you are in known territory.

The rubrics

Everything on your exam paper, apart from the questions themselves, is known as the 'rubrics'. The rubrics include instructions and information.

Read through the rubrics on a past paper for the previous year. Take note of what is covered, such as:
- the name of the exam subject;
- the date;
- the length of the exam;
- where you write your name or a number you have been given;
- how many questions to answer in each section;
- whether you are allowed to use electronic equipment;
- whether you are required to answer in pencil, as for some multiple choice exams;
- any other instructions and information about the exam.

Compare these details with what was written in previous years. You will probably find that the content of the information does not differ much from year to year, but the appearance may vary.

Revision session 1: Familiarity with the exam paper (*continued*)

Time

As you look at past exam papers:

- Note the length of the exam.
- Notice how many questions you are required to answer, and whether these are essays, short answers, or multiple choice.
- Work out how long you have for each question.

Divide the total exam time between the number of questions you have to answer, giving equal time to questions that carry the same marks. For example:

- If 80% of the exam is essays, then 80% of the time should be spent on essays.
- If 50% of the exam is short answers, spend 50% of your exam time on these.
- If there are 3 essays to write in 3 hours, spend about an hour on each.
- If there are 4 essays to write in 3 hours, spend about 45 minutes on each.
- If there are 12 short answers to write in 2 hours, spend about 10 minutes on each.

How much can you write in the time?

Before you go into an exam, you should know how much you can write in the time available. You then know how much or how little you can write for each main point you wish to make.

Check your writing speed

- Choose a topic you can write about for 15 minutes, such as a sport, a TV programme, a place you have visited.
- Set an alarm clock for 15 minutes' time.
- Write non-stop, as quickly as you can, until the alarm sounds.
- Count the number of words you wrote.
- Multiply this number by 4 to see how many words you could write in an hour.

Revision session 1: Familiarity with the exam paper (*continued*)

How many words per paragraph?

- Divide the total number of words you calculated that you could write in an hour by 10 (roughly the number of paragraphs you will write).
- For an essay of 10 paragraphs, therefore, you would have this many words for each paragraph, or main section of your argument.
- Return to the writing you produced in 15 minutes (p. 144). Count out the words that you have calculated are available to you for each paragraph, and draw a line under the text at this point.
- The writing above the line is roughly the amount of words, in number and visually, that you will have in the exam to make each key point.
- When you are in the exam, you should aim to make each key point in roughly that amount of text, in order to ensure you cover all the points you need to make.

Revise what you can produce

When you are revising, aim to reduce the amount of information you are revising to roughly the amount you can use, realistically, in the exam. Use the amount you can write as an indicator of what you should revise.

Refresh your memory

Read through pages 87–8, in 'What are examiners looking for?' Consider how that applies to the questions on the exam paper you are using.

Identify the key question words

- For one topic, write out a list of all the questions that have come up on past papers so far.
- Look through your list and note how the questions are worded. Look for patterns in the kinds of questions set. For example, for this topic, do the questions usually tend to require description, explanation, summary, analysis, comparisons, or application of information to new situations?
- Look at the wording for questions that are set for other topics on the paper. Consider whether you can use similar wording to invent further questions on your chosen topic that have not appeared so far on past papers. For example, if lots of questions are worded, 'To what extent . . . ', then consider what kinds of 'To what extent' questions could be set for your topic.

Revision session 2: Sort material

About this session

Information gathered throughout the term, semester or year is not usually organised in a way that best suits our exam preparation. Organising a better system can, in itself, help us to become better acquainted with the material and to recall it. You may find it helpful to read the 'Building knowledge architectures' section (in Chapter 8, p. 136) as part of this revision session.

Motivation

The motivation for this session is making your course material more manageable for exam purposes.

Focus

Using previous exam papers, read quickly through the exam questions that were set on one topic over the last few years. Jot down a quick list of the main variations. Add other variations of your own to these questions if you think they are realistic alternatives for your exam. This will help you to organise your thinking, and to make decisions about the information you really need.

Gather

Bring together your paper and electronic notes on the subject, and any books where you have written notes against the text or highlighted information.

Sift

● Go through your notes and texts, bearing in mind the likely exam questions you listed above.
● Select those items, from your various sources, that are most useful to those questions.
● Put aside any notes that duplicate information, and put aside time later to reduce these down to one overall set of notes without duplications.
● Ask yourself questions such as:
  – Am I really likely to use this?
  – For which questions would I use this information?
  – How much of this material would I be able to include, given the word limits?
  – What are the most essential points?

Revision session 3: Reduce down and organise

About this session

Having too many notes, and disorganised notes, wastes your time in searching through unnecessary material and learning things you won't use. You can revise the essential material more effectively if it is clearly laid out and organised.

Motivation

Set yourself challenges, such as:

● reducing your notes down to a much smaller number of pages;
● allowing yourself a maximum number of pages or cards per topic;
● setting time limits for organising a certain number of pages.

Reduce

Decide on methods for cutting down your information to only that material you are likely to use under exam conditions. This is usually much less than for coursework. You may require several revision sessions to condense your notes, using one or more of the methods listed here.

Methods for reducing information

1 Rewrite different sets of notes into one shorter set of key points and headings.
2 Incorporate into your notes the material you have underlined or highlighted in books.
3 Set yourself a limited total number of pages of notes per topic (for example, 1 page) and stick to this.
4 Write notes as a series of key headings, with a few key points under each.
5 Write out your notes again as answers to likely exam questions, choosing only information that is really relevant to each question.
6 Produce a series of cards, each bearing key information on one topic (p. 149).
7 Draw a chart or diagram of the key information for each topic (p. 272).

Organise

As you cut down material into one set of notes, organise it so it is easy to use when you go through it next time. For example:

● Is it easy to read?
● Is it well labelled?
● Do the headings relate to likely topics for paragraphs for exam questions?
● Can you use colour to make key points stand out better or to link different topics?
● Are points numbered sensibly?

Revision session 3: Reduce down and organise
(*continued*)

Tip

It is generally easier to remember information that is organised as a series of headings, with key information listed as numbered bullet points beneath these.

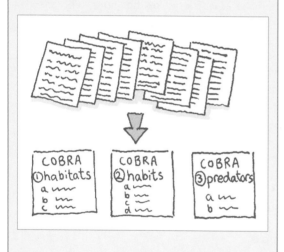

Tip

As you reduce down your notes, monitor whether you are including more detail than you could use in an exam. If so, either:

● remove information you are not likely to use in the exam; or

● score a line through it so you have a visual reminder of the less important material.

Preparing for the hunt

As you reduce your course material, note any gaps in your knowledge. Make a point of hunting out this information within the next few days, while the revised subject is still fresh in your mind. This will help you to remember the overall topic in a coherent way.

Hunt List

1. Who wrote . . . ?
2. Date of . . .
3. How does X work?
4. Make notes for lecture I missed on Y.

Revision session 4: Prepare one exam question

About this session

This session builds on the previous two structured revision sessions. The aim is to prepare one exam question. This gives you practice in organising material and helps you identify material you already have for a typical exam question and to spot gaps in your knowledge and understanding.

Resources

You will need:
- 12 index cards or blank postcards,
- several past exam papers,
- your reduced notes on the topic.

Motivation

The motivation for this session is that the question you work on may be very similar to one that appears in the exam.

Focus

- Choose one topic for the session.
- Read at least twice through several past exam questions, noting the questions for the topic you selected.

- Note whether any types of question appear on more than one paper.
- Select one question and use that as a focus for the revision session.

Consider the title

Read the essay title carefully, considering what kind of answer is required. If you are not used to analysing exam questions, see pp. 89–93.

Sum up: Index card 1

- On the first index card, write out the question, so you can see easily the focus of this set of cards.
- Consider what your overall answer will be and sum this up in 2–3 lines beneath the title on the first card. At this stage, you may find it helpful to do this in pencil, so you can improve your summary later.
- On the back of index card 1, jot down a list of up to 9 possible paragraph topics, and add 'Introduction' and 'Conclusion' to your list (see p. 150).

As you prepare your answer, return to these key points and add in the main research references you will need for the exam.

Revision session 4: Prepare one exam question
(*continued*)

Index card 1 (front)

Exam question

To what extent was X successful in achieving Y?

Summary of argument

X was largely successful at A, B and C, and partially successful in attaining D. These successes meant that the first stage of Y was achieved. However, X failed to achieve E and F. As E and F were the most significant aspects of Y, overall X was unsuccessful in achieving Y.

Index card 1 (reverse)

Proposed list of paragraphs, with references

1　Introduction
2　Why X wanted to achieve Y
3　Key stages and aspects of Y
4　Reasons why X can be considered to have achieved A (Mullins, 2004)
5　Reasons why X can be considered to have achieved B and C (Lacey, 1999)
6　Why D can be considered a partial achievement of Y (Begum, 2005)
7　Reasons why X can be considered not to have achieved E and F (Makelele, 2000)
8　Reasons why some people argue X did achieve E (Lacey, 2002)
9　Reasons why these arguments are not convincing (Makelele, 2004)
10　Reasons why E and F are the most significant aspects of Y
11　Other important considerations
12　Conclusion

Revision session 4: Prepare one exam question
(*continued*)

Check for relevance

Reread the question. Check that your list of proposed paragraphs are all relevant to the question selected. If not, then review these.

Look for gaps

Look quickly through your set of reduced notes and see if you have missed any key reasons that are relevant to your argument. If so, add these to your list.

Hunt for additional information

If you are not sure whether you have really covered all essential angles, you may wish at this stage to look back to your full set of notes. Check quickly through textbooks, using the index, to find further information.

Amend the paragraphs list

As you gather any additional information, you may wish to amend your list of proposed paragraphs. Check that these are still all relevant to the question.

Note key points for each paragraph

Once you are happy with your list of probable paragraphs, it is time to fill in the detail. At the top of 9 of the remaining 11 cards, write a heading that sums up the focus of each potential paragraph. On each card, under the heading, jot down a legible list of the main points you would include in that paragraph, including any relevant names, dates or essential data.

Be succinct

In the exam, you won't be able to write very much for each paragraph or stage in your argument. This is why it is useful to have only one small card to write out the key information. Avoid:

- adding in additional cards;
- using very large cards;
- using tiny writing so you can include more.

If there seems a lot to say, consider how to pare this down to the most essential aspects. This will:

- help you to recall the information later;
- give you valuable practice in editing;
- save you time thinking through what to leave out if this question or a similar one comes up in the exam.

Write an introduction and conclusion

Use the two final cards to draw up the main points you will include in your introduction and conclusion.

Revision session 5: Preparing multiple answers

About this session

This session builds on session 4, developing skills in identifying the exact requirements of each exam question, and applying information differently depending on what is asked.

Motivation

The motivation for this session is that you will have prepared one topic from several angles. Even if none of these questions appear in the exam exactly as you revised them, working in this way helps your understanding and recall of the material overall, increasing your ability to answer any exam question on the topic.

Focus

Read through the cards you prepared for session 4.

Choose five exam questions

Choose up to five exam questions from previous exam papers, all closely related to the essay you prepared in session 4. Add your own variations by:

- applying question words that were used for other topics on past exam papers;
- covering interesting new material from recent seminars or journal articles.

Consider the title

Read the essay title carefully, considering what kind of answer is required. Note the exact wording. Make a brief list of the ways the answer to this question would be similar to that for session 4. List the ways it would be different.

Sum up: Index card 1

- On the first index card, write out the question, just as you did in session 4.
- Consider what your overall answer will be and sum this up in 2–3 lines beneath the title. At this stage, you may find it helpful to do this in pencil, so you can change your mind later.
- On the back of index card 1, jot down a list of up to 9 paragraph topics, and add 'Introduction' and 'Conclusion' to your list.

Compare your list

Compare your list of possible paragraph headings for this question with the one you produced for session 4. How do they differ? How far does this reflect differences in the way the exam questions are worded?

Revision session 5: Preparing multiple answers (*continued*)

Selective recycling

- Consider carefully how far you can use any of the cards you have already prepared for session 4.
- If some of the material you used in session 4 is also suitable for the question you are now preparing, then either copy the material out again on the cards you are preparing for this question or, to save time, simply write a reference to it on the relevant cards for this essay, with a note of any differences you might want to make.
- If the information you need for this essay is not identical to that used in a previous essay, then write new cards for this essay, containing only information that is relevant.
- Check for any additional information you might need to answer this particular question.
- Continue to fill out a full set of index cards for your paragraphs, as for session 4.

Repeat the activity

- Choose another question on this topic.
- Go through the above activity, noting similarities and differences between the questions, and seeing which material applies to more than one question.

- Note the differences between the three essays as well as the similarities.
- Consider which cards, or details on specific cards, would be suitable for one question but not another.

Repeat the activity

Repeat this activity with further questions on this for as long as you find it useful and necessary to continue.

> **Tip**
> Select information wisely to answer the set question. Beware of repeating information from the previously prepared essays if it is not necessary to answer the particular question set.

Once you have considered several questions on the same or related topics, it is likely that you will feel that you understand how that subject is examined, and also that you can work more flexibly with the material relevant to that topic without feeling you have to repeat the same information for every question.

Revision session 5: Preparing multiple answers
(*continued*)

Chart the differences

Now that you know the variations on the kinds of questions that can come up for the topic, draw up a chart of the similarities and differences so you can see these links or contrasts at a glance. For example:

Topic/question	Exam question 1	Exam question 2	Exam question 3	Exam question 4
Economic gains are a benefit	X		X	
Damage to environment	X	X		
Regeneration benefits	X		X	
Regeneration benefits over-estimated	X	X	X	
Positive community development	X		X	X
Positive cultural development			X	X
Growth in the arts generally			X	X
Marine-related arts development			X	X
Damage caused to marine life		X		
Sea coast protection (to people)	X	X		
Sea coast protection (marine life)		X		
Marine life development (example)	X	X		
Local ecosystems developed	X	X		X
Challenge to notion of ecosystems development	X	X		

Revision session 6: Practice questions and mock exams

About these sessions

Although doing practice papers may never feel exactly like doing the real exams, there is still a great deal to be gained by doing them. You will gain:

- more awareness of how you perform under time pressures;
- time to reflect on your performance and identify areas for improvement.

Motivation

You will find out whether there are areas where you need to improve, so you can work on this in advance of the exam. Knowing you have done this should boost your confidence on the day of the exam.

Arrange your 'exam space'

Set aside a space for your mock exam that is as similar to exam conditions as possible:

- a table cleared of everything except an exam paper, writing materials, and water;
- where you can easily see the time;
- where you won't be interrupted;
- where you won't be tempted to go and look up anything that you have forgotten;
- with no distractions such as TV or music.

Practice questions and mocks

When you have revised a topic, it can be useful to put aside an hour to practise one question.

- Choose a topic you have prepared.
- Set the alarm so it will sound when the time you would have in the exam is up.
- Read the question and prepare a quick outline plan to structure your answer.
- Write out your answer in full, without abbreviations or 'texting', and with an introduction and conclusion.
- Work as quickly as you can, leaving a few minutes to check your answer.
- Stop as soon as the alarm sounds.

Revision session 6: Practice questions and mock exams (*continued*)

'Open book' exams

If you have 'open book' exams as part of your course, or if you are not used to exams, then you may find it helpful, at first, to work with your reduced notes in front of you. If you really can't remember something, then you can check your notes. Looking material up takes time, so if your actual exam is not 'open book', give yourself additional time equivalent to the time you spent searching for information.

Practise without 'looking up'

Aim to practise writing out answers to exam questions without checking anything, even if you have open book exams. The advantages are:

- You will have more motivation to learn the material.
- You will get a better sense of the material you need to remember (see Chapter 8).
- You will be able to write more quickly and continuously in the exam, making better use of the time available.
- You will feel more confident that you can keep going in the exam without the support of written prompts.

Full mock exams

Once you have practised answers for several different topics, it is worth sitting a full 'mock' exam, in conditions as near as possible to those of your future exam. So, for example, if you are required to write 3 essays in 3 hours in your exam, do this in your mock exam too.

Setting

Consider doing your mock exam in a place you do not usually work in, such as a section of the library that is unfamiliar to you. This will help you gain the experience of writing in exam conditions. Choose a place where your friends won't be able to disturb you.

Keep going

Even if you struggle to answer some questions, keep going for the full equivalent of the exam time. If you get stuck, make effective use of the time available:

- visualise your reduced notes,
- use your mnemonics,
- free-associate about the topic,
- check your answers for errors,
- list the things you wish you could remember,
- consider starting a different question.

Revision session 7: Learning from practice

About this session

Practice sessions and mock exams vary greatly in how useful they feel at the time. It is important to keep them in perspective. Think calmly about the experience and consider the practical lessons that can be drawn from them.

Motivation

This session draws together your observations about your exam performance, so you can use future revision sessions to build on your strengths and address areas for improvement.

Timing

Complete a copy of the questionnaire on the following pages soon after you have finished the practice paper or mock exam. Leave a few hours or days so you have time to absorb the experience, and then come back to the questionnaire and see whether you wish to add to, or change, any of your answers.

MOCK EXAM IN PROGRESS

Yes! That was great! I didn't realise I knew so much! What great ideas came to mind! I can do my exams easily!

Mock Exam 2–5

Oh no! I ran out of time! I couldn't remember anything! My tummy kept rumbling I was so hungry. I have to plan better for the real exam!

Revision session 7: Learning from practice
(*continued*)

Aspect	Observations on your exam performance	Comments
Are you better at some question types than others? For example, were you drawn towards 'Compare and contrast' type questions, or 'Explain' questions rather than those starting: 'To what extent'?		Consider what it is you find more challenging about the question types you prefer less, and how you can make these questions seem easier. Practise working on those question types you like least, to build your confidence and skills, and to give yourself a wider range of questions to choose from in the exam.
Which memory strategies worked best for you? For example, did you find it easier to remember information that you had talked through, that was in your reduced notes or index cards, or that you had used a technique to recall? What sort of information did you forget to include and how will you remember it in future?		Use practice sessions to find out which memory techniques work for you. For example, if you remembered material from seminar discussions, then arrange to talk through your subject with other students and try other auditory methods (p.130). If you remembered only the colour or shape of mindmaps and diagrams but not their content, then don't rely on such diagrams alone to jog your memory – use verbal or tactile memory joggers too.

Revision session 7: Learning from practice (*continued*)

Aspect	Observations on your exam performance	Comments
Did you choose the right questions? Did you wish you had selected different questions once you started to write?		Consider how you will avoid this mistake in the future. Do you need more practice in answering that kind of question? Do you need to revise further aspects of the topic so you can answer a greater range of questions on it? Do you need to spend more time before or during the exam working out what is required for each question?
Did you answer questions in the best order for you? For example, did you do your best question first or last, and did this work? What, if anything, did you wish you had done differently about the order you answered questions?		Experiment with writing your best question first, to see if this builds your confidence. Would you be better starting with your worst question in order to get it out of the way? If you leave your weakest choice until last, you may develop more ideas about it during the rest of the exam. It is best not to leave your best question until last, in case you run out of time. Practise different approaches to see which works for you.
Can you tell how good it is? Do you need an objective opinion?		Swap practice exam answers with a student on your course, or ask a friend for feedback.

Revision session 7: Learning from practice (*continued*)

Aspect	Observations on your exam performance	Comments
Did you time the practice session well? Did you spend roughly equal time on questions that gain the same marks? Did you leave sufficient time to finish all questions, including writing introductions and conclusions? Did you have sufficient time to check over your work? Did you feel you were in control of the time?		For future practice sessions, write out the exact times you will start and finish each question, and factor in time for reviewing your answers. Experiment with writing less in each paragraph, by making your points more succinctly. Check whether certain aspects such as opening sentences or conclusions are taking you too long. If so, practise these separately.
Writing speed? Did you feel that you were being held back by not being able to write quickly enough?		If your writing speed is slow, you can improve this by practising writing at speed each day – such as by writing out a practice answer at speed. You need to gain a feel of how much you can write in an exam, and how you will allocate the number of words you are able to write to the key points you wish to make (see p. 144). Consider whether you are too ambitious in how much you wish to include and, if so, what you could cut out.

Revision session 7: Learning from practice
(*continued*)

Aspect	Observations on your exam performance	Comments
Read through your practice answers. Is your line of reasoning, or main argument, very clear?		If not, consider whether you have worked out sufficiently what your position is on the issues raised by the subject. Rewrite sections of the essay to make your arguments stand out more clearly.
Did you write an essay plan and keep to it? Are your answers clear and focused, with one point following logically from another? Or do your answers 'hop around' and lack clear direction?		Some people can plan in their heads, but consider whether your answers are sufficiently organised and structured. Practise writing quick essay plans, numbering your key points in the optimum order.
Do your answers contain some or all of the items listed on p. 87, where relevant?		Look over your answers again and see where you could change them to include characteristics that would boost your marks.
Did you struggle writing opening and closing sentences, introductions and conclusions?		Practise writing several variations of these, building your speed and skill. You may be able to adapt basic versions of these in the exam.
Are your answers legible and free of careless errors?		Proofread your work again and see if you find any further errors or illegible words that could have lost you marks.

Closing comments

Summary Key points

- ★ Plan out the time for each revision session.
- ★ Familiarise yourself with typical exam papers.
- ★ Write as many practice answers as you can.
- ★ Condense and organise material so it is easier to absorb.
- ★ Summarise answers and arguments on index cards.
- ★ Practise writing introductions and conclusions.
- ★ Organise material flexibly to draw on for different questions.
- ★ Set yourself a mock exam to identify where you could improve your strategy.

The sessions above provide a structured way of managing information that you have accumulated over your course of study, and using this to answer exam questions in conditions similar to those you will encounter in the exam.

If you found it hard to focus when completing practice papers, this is likely to improve under real exam conditions. If you are concerned about lack of focus, then plan out your answers and follow the plans through. If you found some questions difficult when you tried them under exam conditions, then don't abandon them at once. Having worked on them already, you may simply need to do some additional work in order to gain a better grasp of the subject. However, if the subject remains difficult, then you may have discovered that this is not an ideal one for you to depend on as a choice in the exam.

It is useful to draw up several outline essay plans on one topic, looking at the same subject from different perspectives and in relation to other topics that could be combined into a single exam question. This not only builds your confidence that you can answer a range of questions on your chosen topics, but such practice reinforces your understanding and recall of the subject.

Revision sessions which focus on working with the material in an interactive way, as suggested in this chapter, are an important part of exam preparation. However, as earlier chapters have emphasised, it is just as important to develop other skills, such as maintaining calm and mental equilibrium in the build-up to the exam. These themes are developed further in the next chapter.

Chapter 10

Stress, health and performance

Learning outcomes

This chapter supports you in:

- recognising signs of stress
- identifying possible causes of stress
- identifying actions you can take to manage stress and anxiety
- developing techniques to create mental calm
- understanding the links between health, stress and performance

Stress affects most students for some of the time. That is to be expected and we shouldn't worry about having some nerves, anxiety or even occasional feelings of being overloaded. These are normal parts of the student experience, especially around exam times and when other assessments are due.

Increased stress, in the short term, can help us to perform well. One aspect of managing stress is to keep it in perspective, rather than letting nerves distract us from our main objectives.

However, if stress is maintained at high levels, then our health as well as our intellectual functioning will be affected. It can then become increasingly hard to cope with any aspect of life, and not just exams. Such stress can build up over time, without us realising that we are coping less well with its effects. In the longer term, the effects can be very serious, even though we may not notice them in the short term.

On the other hand, taking care of our physical and mental health can, in itself, keep stress under control and contribute to better exam performance. This chapter emphasises the importance of monitoring your own stress levels, recognising when you are feeling over-anxious, and taking action to manage your stress and anxiety levels.

Identifying stress early can help you to manage it before it starts to undermine your performance or affect your well-being.

Useful levels of stress

Even if you are interested, motivated and confident about your exams, you may be carrying more stress than is helpful.

What is stress?

Our minds can interpret anxiety as a sign that we are under threat from an external force. Our bodily protective systems are generally very strong, and so a sense of 'emergency' can trigger our minds to think we need to take action to protect ourselves. The body takes steps to help us ward off the potential external danger, and some of these physiological changes are also useful for academic performance:

● a little stress is energising;
● adrenalin is released to increase our ability to function;
● blood is diverted from bodily functions to the brain and large muscles;
● our breathing changes so we take in more oxygen to help us function;
● the liver releases stored sugars, so we feel we have more energy.

Stress or excitement?

The chemicals released in the body and our physiological responses when we are stressed are similar to those associated with excitement. The difference is how we experience this: our minds provide an interpretation of whether we are feeling excited or anxious.

Stress can help performance

Most performers claim that they feel anxious before they go on stage. There is a moment when they fear that they may not be able to face the public, that they will forget their lines or be unable to move or sing. However, after many performances, they know that a certain level of nervous anxiety is useful. It adds the edge to their performance. Similarly, when you need to perform well in exams, it helps if you can acknowledge your nerves as useful friends. The adrenalin release can:

● provide the energy that enables you to do the extra work needed;
● make you more alert so you can take in more information;
● keep you focused for longer.

Reflection

Do you tend to regard all stress and nervous anxiety as bad?

Have you noticed any times when you have benefited from nerves or stress?

Unhelpful levels of stress

Although some stress is useful, and stress is a typical aspect of the student experience, too much stress is unhealthy, undermines our performance, and, over time, can have very serious effects. 'Too much' stress includes:

1 **Too much at once**   There are just too many things to cope with at once. To reduce the stress, you have to reduce the number of things you are working on at present, or devote effort to managing the stress.

2 **Too long**   The short-term response suitable for a 'state of emergency' can become a way of life. The mind and body may need to be trained out of this response.

Check for signs of stress

Use the checklist on p. 166 to identify whether you are showing signs of high stress levels.

The impact of high stress?

If the 'state of emergency' continues for a long time, then our systems start to become overwhelmed by the chemicals released, and our functioning starts to deteriorate, or even stops.

Impaired academic performance

If stress levels are too high, it is hard to maintain concentration, our attention wanders, we find it hard to settle down to study. Memory can be affected, and at times we may not be able to recall even information we know really well. It becomes harder to plan and to find solutions to problems.

Impaired physical health

Over time, high levels of the chemicals associated with stress can damage body tissues and organs. At a basic level, just grinding our teeth can wear them away and give us jaw pain or extreme headaches that make it hard to sleep or study. Our immune systems can be affected, making us prone to illness.

Impaired mental health

If stress levels are maintained for long periods, we can start to lose our ability to function in everyday life. Sleep is affected, which impairs performance and also our ability to perceive the world around us accurately. Our perspective can become distorted, and we can experience panic attacks, depression or helplessness.

Social impact

Stress can make it difficult for us to be around other people: they can seem very irritating or deliberately obstructive. It can be hard to feel affection for those we are close to, and we can become irritable or emotional quickly, so that it is hard for other people to be with us.

Check for signs of stress: Behaviours and emotions

Stress checklist

Indicate whether the following apply (Yes/No) and then tick the boxes that apply to you.

Stress indicator	Yes/No	mild change	big change	steady increase	sudden increase
Are you unusually irritable, angry or aggressive?					
Do you feel anxious, worried or agitated?					
Do other people seem more annoying than usual?					
Is it hard to feel or maintain affection at present?					
Are you eating without noticing what you eat?					
Are you drinking more alcohol than usual?					
Do you need alcohol or drugs in order to cope?					
Are you engaging in comfort behaviours (eating, drinking, shopping, excess exercise) to cope?					
Are you more clumsy or ineffective than usual?					
Are you becoming emotional very easily (e.g. angry, tearful, snapping or shouting at others)?					
Do you find yourself often worrying that you can't get through all you need to do?					
Are you finding it harder than usual to concentrate, think clearly or make decisions?					
Are you more forgetful or disorganised than usual?					
Are you missing deadlines and appointments?					

Check for signs of stress: Physical

Stress checklist

Indicate whether the following apply (Yes/No) and then tick the boxes that apply to you.

Stress indicator	Yes/No	mild change	big change	steady increase	sudden increase
Are you losing sleep?					
Are you sleeping longer and finding it harder to get up?					
Do you feel you need to take stimulants (coffee or drugs) to stay awake or concentrate?					
Are you repeatedly catching minor ailments, such as colds and infections?					
Do you have many headaches or migraines?					
Are you grinding your teeth (or finding that your jaw or back teeth are aching)?					
Do you frequently feel very tired or exhausted?					
If you have asthma or allergies, are your attacks new, worse or more frequent?					
Are skin complaints new, worse or more frequent?					
Do you have frequent stomach or bowel upsets, not obviously linked to diet?					
Have you lots of aches and pains, unrelated to obvious illness?					

Am I stressed?

Consider the accuracy

If you have completed the checklist on pp. 166–7, consider your responses:

- Are your answers accurate?
- Did you avoid ticking some items because you were embarrassed?
- Were you tempted to provide any false answers because you were concerned about the pattern of your responses?
- Did you tick any items because today is an unusually bad day?

Reflection  **Characteristics of stress**

Look at the items that you ticked. For each of these, consider:
- How serious is this characteristic?
- What is its impact on you and your life?
- Is it something you need to address straight away?

Few signs of stress?

If you didn't identify many signs of stress, and you are generally regarded as a calm or easy-going person, then that is good. You may wish to consider:

- Would you benefit from taking action to maintain your state of calm?

- Do you build up enough excitement and bring sufficient energy to your study and revision in order to perform at your best?
- If you don't already have outlets for your stress, are you bottling it up?

Expected signs of stress?

If you identified many signs of stress, you may recognise that this has been building up for some time. If so, you need to do something now to make your stress more manageable.

Stressed without knowing it?

You may be unpleasantly surprised to find you are showing a number of signs of stress, and feel that you would know best if you were really stressed. If so, at least be open to the possibility that you may benefit from reducing your current levels of stress.

It is possible to be stressed, and even very stressed, without being aware of this. Stress can creep up on us over time, and we learn to live with its effects to some extent. However, underlying stress may be taking its toll on our health and well-being. It can be useful simply to acknowledge that you may be feeling stressed and to engage in some form of relaxation or exercise to reduce overall stress levels.

Take action to manage stress

Identify the causes

If you have identified signs of stress, and acknowledged that you are feeling unwanted levels of stress, then the next stage is to identify the causes and do something to change these.

For example, you may feel that 'exams' in general are to blame, whereas it is more likely to be something specific in the way you think about exams and approach them that generates unnecessary stress.

Unrealistic goals?

Unrealistic goals are a frequent cause of exam stress. For example, you may be so determined to achieve a certain grade that you are neglecting other things that you value. You are more likely to achieve your own peak performance if you set yourself a goal that is challenging but realistic for your circumstances.

Consider whether you are setting yourself realistic aims, given:

- the time you have at your disposal;
- what you have achieved in the past;
- what other people could realistically achieve in the same time;
- the skills and knowledge you have already gained in this subject compared with those you have still to acquire.

Focusing on problems?

Are you feeding your own anxiety by letting yourself dwell on problems? If so, there are things you can do to change the shape of your thinking: see 'Getting in "the zone" (i)', p. 29.

Poor care of your health?

You can reduce stress by taking care of your health: eating and sleeping well, avoiding excess coffee, tea, cigarettes, sugar and red food dyes (see p. 200). You may have food sensitivities that can contribute to feeling stressed and irritable. If you think this is possible, then you could benefit from a food sensitivity test.

Take action

- If you notice a change in your health, talk to a doctor about this.
- Use exercises and activities such as those on the following pages to manage your stress levels.
- If you worry about time pressures, speak to your personal tutor or equivalent: they may be able to offer study strategies.

Students' experiences

I get really nail-bitingly nervous several weeks before my exams. What do I do? Apart from biting my nails, mostly talking to my mom on the phone. She always helps me get my feet on the ground.

I get on the bus and look out of the window: it makes me day-dream and I feel more relaxed when I get back.

I do have mega exam anxiety. I spend hours worrying, and then I worry that I'm worrying, and then I blame myself for wasting time worrying. None of it gets me anywhere, but it fills the hours so I feel I have done something. Well, I'm not so bad since I started yoga. The class is very calming and the regular break does me good. It's calming being away from student life for a while.

Music. I put on my headphones, choose something really wild, and turn it up loud. I might even dance along if no one else is in.

I went to the Student Services office about money, but ended up talking about everything else. They recommended 3 sessions with a counsellor. I wouldn't go at first as I thought it meant admitting failure. I only went because I found out my friend had gone. It was the best thing I could have done. They helped me work out for myself what I needed to do, so I felt I had more space to think.

I don't think I have ever felt stressed. People keep asking me if I am but I don't know why. Maybe I seem stressed.

My stress levels kept going up and I did cope fine, but I felt miserable all the time. All my time was being swallowed up with work, worry and study, but I had to so something different. Now, I make sure I get to do 2 or 3 things a week that are just for enjoyment – it's not so much what I do as recognising that I have stopped study and work and this is time for me. I think I am more efficient in the way I do things, so things are better all round.

Running: I run a mile a day and that clears my system of worry and leaves me clear-headed.

Reflection

What lessons could you learn from these students' experiences?

© Stella Cottrell (2006, 2012) *The Exam Skills Handbook*, Palgrave Macmillan

Working off anxiety

Work off the adrenalin

As we saw above, a certain amount of stress is useful as it produces adrenalin, which keeps you alert and focused. However, excess adrenalin can make you feel anxious, making it hard to maintain attention. Physical activity can help work off the excess adrenalin, making it easier to feel calm again.

If you are not used to exercise, going for a brisk walk for about half an hour will do: note the world around you rather than stewing over your worries.

> I AM applying myself to my exam preparation. Revision strategy 47: working off excess adrenalin.

Avoid 'false friends'

Are the people around you really helping you to feel more relaxed, healthy and in control of your study? If not, seek out friends and family who make you feel calm and relaxed.

> Only 50% of people ever pass this exam, so we'll probably fail.

> There's no point going over your notes at this point – if you don't know it by now, you never will.

> Global warming makes everything irrelevant anyway.

Speak to people who are likely to be reassuring and supportive. Avoid those who are likely to make you feel anxious about the exam, talk doom and gloom, or try to persuade you not to revise.

Calming exercises (1)

The voice of reason

Talk yourself through your worries. Ask yourself 'Questions of reason', such as those below.

Questions of reason

- Am I keeping things in proportion?
- Most people pass exams, so if I work steadily and keep my head, isn't it likely I will too?
- What can I do, practically, to reduce my worry and resolve problems?
- Who can I speak to who will make me feel good about myself and about life? Why not arrange now to meet them soon?
- Who can I speak to who will give me good advice? Why not arrange this right now?
- If the worst-case scenario occurs, what practical options will be open to me? There are always other options.
- It is nice to get outstanding results, but in the longer term, won't a reasonable pass open many doors for me too?
- Do I need a break?

Affirmations

If you tend to be self-critical, or to feel negative about your own performance, then consider one or two sets of words that would make you feel more positive and motivated. A line from a song, or a quotation from someone you admire, may help. Make a point of looking at these, and taking them in, at least twice a day.

Write it large

Write your affirmation in large letters and put it where you can see it when you are revising at home, and where you brush your teeth.

Write it small

Write the affirmations so you can carry them in your purse or wallet, or use them as a bookmark.

Calming exercises (2)

Slow renditions

The aim of this activity is to stop your mind (and pulse) from racing by taking time to find a more reasonable pace.

- Choose a poem, song or chant that you like and know well. Choose a few lines from it.
- Repeat these lines slowly, preferably aloud, and look for pleasure in the sound of the words and the beat.
- If you find you are rushing just to get through it, or that you have repeated the words without taking notice of them, then start again, going more slowly.
- Give yourself permission to take this time to give the words justice.

> I am bee-you-tea-fulllllll
> No matter what marks I gain
> Exams won't bring me-eee downnnn
> Even if I have resits again!

Note the sounds

- Put aside 10–30 minutes so that you have a definite break.
- Lie on the floor, with your head supported, and close your eyes.
- Take notice of your own body. How does it feel? Are there any aches and pains you weren't aware of?
- Working upwards from your toes, ask yourself whether each part of your body, in turn, is feeling tense. If so, think about that part of the body relaxing into the floor and releasing its tension into the air.
- When your body is as relaxed as possible, turn your attention to the sounds around you.
- Don't aim to label the noises, just note them and let them pass.
- Listen for moments of quiet: how do these, or periods of relative quiet, make you feel? Note any moments of tranquillity.
- When you have finished, don't rush straight back into frenetic activity: give yourself time to absorb the experience.

Meditative calm (1)

There are a number of meditative exercises that you can do to help bring about calm.

Formal meditation courses

You may prefer to follow a formal course of meditation. These tend to teach techniques in small classes, over a few weeks. You can then opt to join a larger group. In the class, you are generally trained to sit comfortably and the tutor talks through the stages of the meditation. You practise this in short spells, building to longer sessions as you become more familiar with the meditation. There may be opportunities to say what you experienced.

Meditation classes usually attract a broad range of people and do not generally commit you to any religious involvement or philosophy.

What do you gain from meditation?

People's experiences of meditation vary greatly. If you find it hard to stop your mind from racing, then you are more likely to benefit from meditation. It may take you longer to feel the benefits if you are attached to an image of yourself as a 'fast thinker' or to having a very vivid imagination. Meditation can offer the opportunity to:

- put time aside just to be with yourself and to see what arises in your mind when deprived of external stimulus;
- become more attuned with what you are feeling but not acknowledging in the business of everyday life;
- be more in touch with other people;
- feel calm and serene;
- feel moments of extreme happiness.

Breathing exercise

The following breathing exercise is, in broad outline, the basis of breathing meditations practised by a number of cultures. People can find they become calmer by practising this when they feel tense. For maximum effect, go through the exercise once or twice a day. Over time, this can develop skill in restoring a calm mood very quickly.

This activity is most useful if you don't force any particular outcome: just note what happens.

- Aim to enjoy the 'time out', as a luxury. Consider how often you allow yourself the privilege of just noticing that you are breathing and, therefore, alive.
- Five minutes of relaxed breathing that you watch with interest is better than 30 minutes of forced meditative exercise.

Meditative calm (2)

What to do

- Sit so you are comfortable, but upright and alert. Close your eyes.

- Consider what mood you are in. Don't try to work out the reasons for your mood or feelings: just accept them for now, and move on.

- Note your surroundings: sounds, odours, the feel of the chair or the floor. Accept that is how they are for now, and move on.

- Become aware of how your body feels. If it is uncomfortable, make minor adjustments, accepting some discomfort if necessary.

- Become aware of which parts of your body are moving. If you are moving your hands, feet, head or mouth, relax these into stillness.

- Notice how your chest and stomach rise and fall as you breathe. If your breathing is noisy, aim to be quieter. Otherwise, just accept the way you are breathing for now, rather than trying to change it.

- Notice your out-breaths: how does it feel to breathe out? Don't change the way you breathe. Count your out-breaths, numbering them from 1 to 10, and then start again. If you find you became distracted, note this and just start again from 1.

- After a few minutes, turn your attention to the in-breaths. As before, consider how they feel. Accept that this is how you are breathing today rather than trying to change anything. Count each number in your head, just before taking each in-breath.

- After a few minutes, follow your in-breaths and out-breaths, counting these in whichever way you find easiest.

- Finally, note where the breath first enters your body and focus on that point, in a relaxed and accepting way. Continue until you feel ready to stop.

- Sit still for a while, and then get up slowly.

- Give yourself time to reflect on the meditation.

Closing comments

Summary **Key points**

★ Learn to recognise your own stress signals.

★ Be sensible about taking proper care of your health.

★ Identify ways of working off your anxiety.

★ Find ways of reducing unnecessary stress.

★ Be proactive in finding ways of feeling calmer.

★ Be proactive in avoiding those people and conditions that trigger unnecessary stress.

★ Build your resilience – learn to work effectively with a certain amount of stress.

At its best, academic study should stretch your mind. It is quite typical to feel challenged by your subject and to struggle with aspects that are difficult to understand. It is likely that there will be times when this feels exhilarating and other times when it feels overwhelming. It is better to acknowledge feelings of nervous anxiety and to take action that enables you to move on from these in a constructive way, rather than to pretend that everything is fine when it is not.

You may feel that stress and anxiety are not relevant matters for you. However, it is unlikely that you can go through student life, or life in general, without periods of unwanted worry and anxiety. At such times, it is useful to have techniques for generating mental calm. We can develop them at any time as tools that we can call upon later when needed.

We can influence our anxiety levels by changing our environment. This means taking care of who we socialise with and who we listen to when we are feeling stressed, and noting who makes us feel anxious and who makes us feel more confident about ourselves. Exercise, good food and sufficient rest contribute to a more relaxed and focused state of mind. We can also make our physical environment relaxing and pleasant to be in, so as to improve our mental state of mind.

When the exam arrives, it is invaluable to have mental strategies for returning to a calm state of mind as quickly as possible if the unexpected arises to make us feel nervous or panicked. It can build our confidence to know that we have such strategies to call upon in the exam room, if needed. As stress can impair our exam performance, it is worth developing calming techniques alongside other exam strategies such as memory strategies and exam practice.

Chapter 11

Getting in 'the zone' (iii): Seeing success

Learning outcomes

This chapter supports you in:
- preparing a state of mind that promotes exam success
- identifying how you achieve at your best
- using 'imaging techniques' to help your exam preparation

This chapter builds upon the preparation you have made through the activities and reflection in previous chapters, particularly Chapters 3 and 4. It introduces more advanced techniques for 'imaging' success and building mental routines to use in the lead-up to exams.

You can undertake imaging techniques at any stage of your preparation – you don't have to wait until you have completed previous activities. However, it is better to develop a positive mind-set and a clear sense of your motivation before applying imaging techniques to the later stages of exam preparation.

You may already use methods similar to those outlined in this chapter. Many people daydream about success, and can see themselves in the exam room. However, the difference between those who excel, and those who use similar methods but do less well, tends to lie in the systematic nature of their approach. This chapter focuses on particular ways of envisaging success in each stage of exam preparation, so that you can approach these calmly, confident of achieving your personal best.

Athletes' use of imaging techniques

Experiencing future success

Athletes who achieve 'the zone' describe the vivid anticipation of victory they experience before they start the race. They help bring this about through their pre-competition preparation, having 'lived' in advance the experience of their every step towards the winning line.

This doesn't mean the athletes were clairvoyant. It means that, as they train, they also think through in detail all facets of their preparation and each aspect of the event itself. They see what they want to achieve, and then think through the pathway from:

● the present moment to the winning line;
● the winning line back to the present time.

Considering every circumstance

Athletes often use visualisation or other imaging techniques to 'see' themselves achieving their goal. They consider how they will succeed under the different conditions that might prevail on the day: extreme sun, rainy weather, other athletes around them, noisy crowds, hushed crowds, false starts, a perfect start.

Not just once

Serious athletes won't go through such imaging techniques once, and expect that the work is done. They go through the critical moments over and over. Each time, they are searching for some fine detail that will give them the edge over other competitors. When they find such details, they rehearse them mentally, seeing where they will fit in the sequence of events, and building these into their practice runs.

The advantage on the day

On the day of the competition, such athletes know exactly what they must do. At the start of the race, they don't *hope* they will be first, they can *see* in their mind's eye how they will cross the winning line. They *know* they are going to achieve their personal best and how they will do it. At critical moments, they know exactly which tasks they must perform, and focus on these. Their self-knowledge provides the confidence and self-esteem needed to achieve their goal.

Winning Line

Why use imaging techniques for exams?

We saw, in Chapter 2, that peak performance tends to take place when we have a strong and reasonably based belief that we are up to the task. We can build this belief by seeing the success, feeling it, and talking ourselves into it. If we build the perception that we are in a state to achieve peak performance, based on the recognition of the work we have put into attaining this, then we are more likely to perform at our optimal level, or 'personal best'.

Although exams offer a different kind of challenge, there are students who take a similar approach to exams to that of top athletes towards competition. It is not known how common this is, partly as students who do well are often reluctant to share the secrets of their success.

The winning line?

Students who talk about advance imaging of success describe similar levels of detailed planning and 'thinking through' what they will encounter. The 'winning line' for exams is more personal, and may vary from passing the exam through to gaining the highest marks ever achieved for a paper. You need to decide what would be the 'winning line' for you when you take each exam (see p. 22).

Living the end result

Long before the exam, you can reflect upon each stage in the revision and exam process, bringing a feeling of calm interest and constructive planning to each step. When that stage in the exam process actually arrives, you will have in place a strong mental image that you can draw on, making it easier to stay relaxed, positive and in control.

Imaging techniques

What is 'imaging'?

Imaging is mostly imagination, but it is more than that. Imaging involves:

Imagination: mentally summoning up or creating different circumstances, most of which have yet to take place.

Practical application: applying the imagination not just to the moment you hold a cup, medal or certificate in your hands but to the steps you must go through in order to achieve that moment.

Present application: bringing the imagination to bear on what you must to do to achieve the current stage in your plan and in this moment, rather than using imagination as a pleasant distraction from what you need to do now.

Building routine: unlike imagination used for creative purposes, imaging uses imagination to develop a mental routine. Keeping to the mental routine keeps you focused and on task.

'Imaging' in time

Imaging techniques involve:

1 Recreating the past in the present, so that you can learn from it (see p. 182, 'How did I do that?').
2 Creating the future in your mind's eye.
3 Applying learning from the past to the imagined future.

More than just 'seeing it'

'Imaging' means more than just 'seeing' yourself going about the business of revision, taking exams or passing the winning line. It is an active process of creating a mental game-plan for achieving success. There are specific techniques you can apply to make the process more effective, such as those detailed below.

Use all your senses

You may be familiar with the idea of visualisation, which, as the name suggests, draws mainly on the visual sense. However, imaging draws actively on all your senses so you feel you are 'experiencing in advance' the activity that you are considering. For example:

- Summon up the sounds you are likely to hear around you on the day.
- See the details of the physical space.
- Sense the odours and atmosphere.
- Feel the pen in your hand.
- Mentally rehearse the actions, letting your muscles go through these as far as is possible.
- Mentally rehearse routines for each stage of exam preparation and the exam room.

Imaging techniques (*continued*)

'Not in the audience'

When we imagine a scene, we may see ourselves within the picture, as if we were standing on the outside or in the audience. Imaging is more successful if you can remain 'on the inside' of the experience, looking out from your own vantage point, rather than as if you were watching yourself perform from the audience.

Self-talk

We can use our 'inner voice' to talk through what we need to do:

- Talk through the routines you have set yourself – know these inside out so you don't need to try to remember them.
- Remind yourself of what is on your planning checklists.
- Give yourself encouragement and advice.
- Tell yourself to keep going.
- Advise yourself what to do if you panic in the exam room: prepare a verbal plan in advance of the exam.
- Tell yourself what is enjoyable or interesting about what you are studying.

Compound schema

When we experience an event, we lay down a rough mental pattern or 'schema' of the event. This is like a rough outline of it. Each time we go through a comparable experience, we fine-tune the pattern, adding in details and building up a more complex but subtle understanding of it. It is better not to rely on just one mental outline for taking your exams: consider a variety of possible scenarios. For example:

- Having half an hour less to complete the exam on the day: how would you manage the time available to you?
- Feeling ill on the day: how will you cope?
- You mis-time your first question, taking too long: how will you recoup the time?
- It is hotter or colder than expected in the exam room: how can you plan for this?

Imaging practice

'Imaging', like any other skill, develops with practice. Orlick and Partington (1988) found that Olympic competitors were not necessarily good at using imaging techniques when they first began, but they improved with practice.

You can apply imaging techniques when going about everyday life, but some of the imaging needs to take place as you revise and practise. The following pages provide a framework for starting the imaging process. As you use this, build in details relevant to your circumstances.

As you image each stage, make notes of personal details that were striking or effective. Structure these into your imaging process the next time you think through that stage of exam preparation.

How did I do that?

In Chapter 3, we noted that good self-awareness is a key factor in attaining peak performance – or 'the zone'.

We all learn more from our personal experience if we take the time to reflect upon how we have met, successfully, the challenges that faced us, especially those where it didn't seem at the outset that we would succeed. Usually, we celebrate and move on, whilst much of the learning we could have gained is lost.

In particular, we are not always good at identifying the personal qualities and attributes that helped us in one circumstance and investigating how we could apply these to a new area. Simply asking, 'How did I do that?' can provide us with insights into what works for us.

Reflection 📖 Managing challenge

Put time aside to think through the following questions in detail. Write your responses in your reflective journal or type them up electronically. Be prepared to come back to this and add to your initial thoughts.

1   What is the most challenging event (e.g. exams, competition, dealing with an emergency, giving a speech, being in performance, etc.) that you have been successful in?
2   What enabled you to succeed (e.g. advance planning, keeping your nerve, calming yourself, support from others)?
3   What was the critical moment (e.g. the moment before the curtain went up, the moment you had to make a decision, etc.)? How did you manage that moment?
4   What, if anything, might have made you give up? How did you overcome those factors?
5   What personal qualities and attributes did you draw on and develop through the experience?
6   How could you apply those in your preparation for your exams and in the exam room?
7   What other qualities or attributes would have been helpful to you at that time and in taking exams? How could you develop these further?
8   What else did you learn from the experience that you could apply to taking exams?

A 'different side' to you

Most of us have probably used expressions such as:

'I saw a different side to her'
'It brought out a different side of me'
'With my manager's hat on, I feel . . .'

This indicates that we know there are different aspects, or 'sides', to our characters that we do not draw upon in everyday life. This 'different' side can offer us an alternative set of qualities, perspectives and behaviours.

Finding a different side

If you feel that you are limited by the 'side' of you that is usually in charge when you are preparing for, or taking, exams, consider what 'other sides' of your character you could call upon instead.

Reflection

Remember a time when you showed a different side of yourself.

● When did this take place?
● What was different?
● What characteristics or personal qualities did you demonstrate?
● How did it feel to discover this different aspect of yourself?
● Have you called upon those characteristics since that occasion? If not, why not?

Acting in role

Don't wait in hope that this different side might suddenly appear. Start to call upon that side of yourself, bringing it more to the foreground. By drawing on that aspect of your character more frequently, you will become more confident that you can draw upon the personal characteristics associated with it when you need them.

A different you in the exam room?

Reflection 📖 Finding a 'different side'

Which 'side' of you is in charge when you are preparing for exams? What are its characteristics and personal attributes? Are these a help or a hindrance?

Consider what 'different side of you' might be hidden away that you could call upon. Is this 'side' happier, more confident, sensible, assertive, organised, better able to cope with stress, better at concentrating, more motivated, etc.? Jot down the qualities you would like this 'other side' to have.

Was there a time when that side of you, or those qualities, were more in evidence? If so, what prevents these from coming to the fore now? For example, were there times when you were laughed at for showing those qualities, or rewarded for not being like that?

Jot down the positive or motivating messages that this 'side of you' would give.

Imagine the shoes or hat that this side of you would wear. Imagine wearing these if you find it hard to summon up that side of you.

Practise in role

Practise completing exam answers 'as if' you were in that 'different side' of yourself. Note the differences in your experience.

No 'different side' in evidence?

If you haven't seen much evidence that there is a different side, then:

- Decide which characteristics and personal qualities would be useful to you in exams.
- Imagine a character that would exhibit such characteristics, such as a mythical hero or a character from a book or film.
- Act 'as if' you were that character when you are using imaging techniques and 'self-talk'.

You may feel self-conscious doing this, but have a go anyway. Observe whether talking in a confident or commanding tone helps you to complete what you need to do more effectively.

Finding enjoyment and challenge

We saw in Chapter 3 that those who experience peak performance also enjoy what they do. This doesn't mean that everything they do is enjoyable – it is likely that much of it isn't. However, high achievers look for the enjoyment in the activity or create it for themselves. They know that finding a source of enjoyment in what they do makes it more likely that they will persevere and achieve.

Exam preparation: Where is the enjoyment for me?	Tick if true	What I could do to find enjoyment from one or more of these items. Which 'side' of me do I need to call upon to find this enjoyment?
Learning new things		
Knowing things other people don't know		
Knowing a subject from many different angles		
Seeing links between different parts of the subject		
Becoming an expert in the subject		
Setting targets and beating these		
Tackling difficult subjects		
Becoming completely absorbed in the subject		
Discussing the subject with others		
Knowing I am on track to gain good marks		
People giving me peace and quiet so I can revise		
Other things:		

Revision: The process in your mind's eye

Imagine yourself going over material for your exam. For example:

- In your mind's eye, you see yourself going through the routine you use to settle yourself down to revise. If you haven't a routine, think through now what kind of routine might help, and test this out until you have a routine that works.

- Imagine yourself enjoying the revision process. You are pleased to be getting to grips with the material. Think of at least one time you have really enjoyed learning something, and go over that experience in your mind. Notice how you feel.

- You can hear yourself explaining what you have just learnt to someone who does not understand the subject, finding good examples to illustrate what you mean. Even if you can't hear all the words yet, get a sense of the satisfaction to be gained from explaining a difficult subject so that someone else can understand it.

- You are pleased that you have the chance to think through possible questions and answers in advance. You invent a question for yourself and wonder if the examiner might come up with similar questions.

- You can see yourself applying material that you have learnt to questions set for previous exams, and feel content that you had covered that topic.

- You experience the delight of realising that you have become an expert in a new subject.

Personal details that arise from your first imaging, to use in future imaging:

Your journey to the exam

Imagine travelling to the exam and the kinds of thoughts you will have – all positive.

- Think through the routine you will go through before leaving the house. What will help you feel calm and focused? What is your strategy for remembering everything (see Chapter 12)?

- Travel the journey in your mind's eye, using the transport and route you will take on the day. You are smiling, so your jaw is relaxed. You may be humming a tune that makes you feel good.

- You are well rested and relaxed, so you can think clearly.

- You haven't eaten too much, so you feel alert rather than dozy. You have eaten enough so you are not distracted by hunger.

- You remind yourself of certain key pieces of information, making a final mental check on the areas you are most likely to need. You are not worried: you know it is very likely that you have covered enough material to answer the right number of questions well.

- You are interested to find out what questions have been set, and to tackle these.

- You are keen to demonstrate what you have learnt to your tutors.

- You are pleased that the exam will soon be behind you and you can celebrate.

And the 9 main functions of the liver are . . .

Write encouraging messages to give yourself on the way to the exam. Begin each with 'I can . . .' or 'I am able . . .'

I can . . .

I can . . .

I can . . .

Movement

Think through your body posture as you travel to the building, and into the exam room. Develop a routine for relaxing your body. For example:

- think tall;
- breathe deeply and slowly;
- relax your neck and shoulders;
- relax your jaw: check you are not clenching your teeth;
- relax your facial muscles: smiling helps this relaxation;
- relax your hands and fingers.

Personal details for future imaging:

In the building

In the building where the exam is held

On the way to the exam:

- You remain calm, alert and interested.
- You avoid conversation, conserving your energies.
- You speak only to people who will make you feel good about the exam.
- You are in plenty of time and have with you everything you need, so there are no unnecessary worries.
- You have prepared well for the exam, so you reassure yourself that this exam will be fine.
- You have left plenty of time to find the exam room and you have visited it in advance of the exam so you know exactly where to find it.

Finding your desk

- You know you may need to check a map to locate your desk, and as it often seems harder to find a desk in such situations, you have arrived in good time.
- There is no need to rush.
- If the numbering isn't immediately clear, you take your time to work it out.
- You are calm and unflustered, even if it has taken some time to locate your desk.
- You sit down and wait for the instructions.
- You focus on taking out your pens and maintaining your calm, rather than looking about.

- You check whether your watch is synchronised with the clock in the exam room.
- You are looking forward to starting the paper.

Personal details for future imaging:

The exam paper

Completing the front of the exam paper

- Think through the routine you will use to make sure you cover every section you are supposed to. Are there opportunities to try this out on past papers?
- You listen to the exams officer or invigilator giving you instructions about completing the details on the front of the exam paper.
- You have checked in advance what would be required, such as through looking at past exam papers, so you are able to follow the instructions easily.
- The instructions are not difficult, and cover such matters as your name or exam number, the date, the name or code of the exam, the centre number.
- You are calm but careful, filling in the front of the exam book accurately, reading the instructions carefully, line by line, down the page in a relaxed but focused calm way.

Reading the exam paper

- Consider in detail the routine you will use to read through the exam paper so that you take in what it says and evaluate each question (Chapter 12).
- You have worked on many questions from previous exam papers, so you know how to interpret the questions.

- You are well prepared, so you are quietly confident.
- You breathe slowly, taking in the information.

Personal details for future imaging:

Selecting questions

- Consider in detail the routine you will use to read through each question, so that you take in and evaluate each one (Chapter 12).
- You can remember what makes a good exam answer (Chapters 6, 13 and 14).
- You imagine yourself selecting questions following your planned routine. You feel positive about the choice of questions.
- Some questions may not be worded as you expected, but you are confident that you can draw together material you know in order to write a good answer that addresses the specific question set.
- You are interested in the questions, keen to get started and to show what you know.
- Your breathing is still calm; you are breathing out deeply and slowly.
- Your jaw, facial muscles, shoulders and hands are relaxed.
- You mark those questions that you feel you can answer, with stars or ticks against those you feel most confident about answering.
- You are reading each question slowly and carefully, checking you can answer each section of the ones that interest you the most.
- You underline key words in each of the questions you are considering answering, making sure you are clear what is being asked for.
- You are already keen to start answering the questions, and scribble a few initial ideas down so you don't forget them.

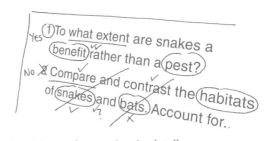

Consider each question in detail.

Personal details for future imaging:

Writing answers

- You see yourself planning out an answer quickly, noting down key points: you are calm and collected. You can almost hear your pen racing across the paper.

- You are thinking about the structure to your answer, the order you will present your material, and how points are linked.

- Your answer provides a well reasoned argument, with good examples and details.

- You note down the time you need to complete the question, so you can keep track of the time available.

- You frame a brief introduction to your answer.

- You are writing answers at a reasonable speed, maintaining your concentration, following your plan.

- You can recall the information that you need, as the answers flow from your pen. If information eludes you, you leave it a moment and carry on with another point, unworried. Before long, you remember the information you wanted.

- You are feeling pleased with your responses and you are enjoying putting the answers together.

- You write a conclusion, linking your argument back to the title, and drawing your answer to a close.

- All your revision is paying off.

Personal details for future imaging:

Finishing the paper

- You have kept your eye on the time and used your exam plan, so you are ready to draw your final answers to a close.
- You have built in enough time to check over your answers for errors and omissions. You do this carefully, making sure the examiner can read what you have written and that your answers make complete sense.
- You are pleased to note some small details that you can add to improve the answer.
- You make the paper look as neat and legible as possible. You have timed this well, so you have just time to finish your checks before you are told to put down your pen.
- You leave the exam room, pleased with your answers and that you have done everything within your power to achieve your best result.

After the exam

- You see yourself leaving the exam room. What are you likely to be feeling: tired? pleased? deflated?
- What do you need most: food? drink? time alone? time with others? to see a film? a treat? a party? time with family?
- Make sure that you plan ahead for different eventualities. It is hard to predict how you will feel after an exam.

Personal details for future imaging:

Closing comments

Summary Key points

★ Approaches used by top athletes can be adapted to achieve exam success.

★ Systematic approaches can help you achieve an optimum mental state.

★ Visualising in detail your way through the process helps you to manage it.

★ Find that part of you that can best succeed at exams.

★ Include all aspects of the process and the day in your imaging of success.

★ Practise these approaches as you would for any skill.

Although having a clear sense of your long-term goals can drive you forward, it is just as important to focus on the immediate tasks that take you towards that goal. This chapter encourages you to image success in the whole process, not just the finishing line.

This chapter assumes that we all have qualities and attributes that we do not necessarily call upon either in everyday life or in our approach to exams. For some of us, these may be demonstrated in different circumstances, but we are simply not applying them to our exam preparation. For others, it may be that helpful qualities were suppressed at some stage in our development.

We can help increase the chances of bringing these characteristics into the foreground by reflecting on which qualities we think we need and then considering where we have demonstrated these in our lives. If the qualities seem alien to us, then we can develop them by acting 'as if' they were part of us, and practising them in our exam preparation.

It is helpful if we can find or develop a side of ourselves that is prepared to look for the enjoyment and interest in exam preparation; that can warm to the challenge, and put the effort into systematic imaging of the exam process. By thinking through the process, considering and planning for obstacles in advance, and experiencing the path towards success, we can build the confidence and capability for a more successful exam outcome.

Chapter 12

The exam

Learning outcomes

This chapter supports you in:
- managing your time effectively before the exam
- undertaking emergency revision measures if you started your revision late
- making final preparations for the exam
- using exam time effectively
- selecting and answering questions
- finding answers to frequently asked questions
- learning from the exam to improve future performance

As the exam approaches, some people will be making their final preparations, whilst others will be trying to make up for lost time. Whichever category you fall into, this chapter can help you with your last-minute preparations. Previous chapters prepare you for these final phases of the revision stage. If you have used these as part of your psychological preparation, don't stop now. Continue to build on the strategies and techniques you have been developing in order to increase your chances of gaining peak performance.

As you become more anxious or preoccupied about the exam, it is easy to forget basic everyday details that you would normally remember. The planning checklists in Appendix 5 (p. 266) can help you to keep track of what you need to do.

You may find it helpful to use this chapter alongside previous chapters, such as Chapter 9, 'Structured revision sessions', on sitting practice exam papers. Imaging techniques from Chapter 11, and relaxation and calming techniques from Chapter 10, can help you prepare the right state of mind for taking your exams.

It is also worth thinking through what you will need, realistically, when the final exam is over – and how you will use this set of experiences in your preparation for any future exams.

Last-minute revision: The time factor

'I haven't enough time left'

It may be the case that you do not have as much time left as you would like. However, it is likely that you have time to do something, so focus on using the time you have left effectively, rather than wasting it in worry. Whatever you do is better than doing nothing at all.

Check your motivation for worrying about time:

● Are you using the resulting anxiety to help you to stay focused?
● Are you overworking?
● Is the worry preventing you from getting down to study?
● Are you using the anxiety as an excuse not to get down to revision?

'I can't cover all the topics'

Check whether you really need to revise every subject. For some types of exam such as multiple-choice and short-answer questions, you do benefit from covering the whole syllabus. However, many exams give you a choice of questions, so you can do well without revising everything.

Leaving subjects out is a risky strategy, so aim to cover at least twice as many topics as you think you will need.

'Don't put all your eggs in one basket'

You are more likely to benefit from revising several subjects in less depth than one or two subjects in great detail. It is generally easier to gather sufficient marks to pass if you answer the required number of questions than if you produce outstanding answers for too few questions.

'I really haven't much time left to prepare!'

If time is really short, use techniques that force you to work at speed:

☐ Give yourself only 5 minutes to jot down a quick list of key topics you need to revise.

☐ Give yourself 5 minutes, maximum, to put these in rough order of importance and of the likelihood they will come up in the exam.

☐ Draw a ring around 2–3 that you feel you know best, or that are least difficult for you. Start revising with these to build your confidence. If you think you know them well enough, then move on to the next topic on your list.

☐ Consider the emergency revision measures outlined below.

Emergency revision measures

If you have left your revision much later than you would wish, then these emergency measures can help.

Gain an overview

Read *quickly* through your notes or a summary of the topic in a textbook, if necessary. The aim isn't to memorise the details, but to get the gist of the topic. This will give you an idea of the bigger picture, and help you to make better use of background information in the exam.

Select key information

- For each topic, identify 2–3 of the key pieces of research.
- Note the name of the person and/or school associated with the research. Picture the names written down, and/or repeat them 3 times each to help you remember them.
- Note the order these pieces of research appeared. Were they linked? Did one lead to another?
- Consider why the research was significant: state this out loud so you hear yourself stating the significance.
- Repeat this at least 3 times, in summary if necessary, to help reinforce the information in your memory.

Move on

- Repeat the above for several topics. This will give you something concrete you can refer to for several subjects.

Return for more

- If you have time, go back and learn a bit more about each topic, starting with the most important.
- Link new information you are revising to material you learnt earlier, to help you organise it mentally.

Use spare moments

- Keep course information close to you and glance over it while you are doing other things, such as making breakfast, dressing, or waiting for the bus.
- Compose answers in your head while you are travelling from one place to another, and check any missing details as soon as possible afterwards.

Last-minute revision: Fine-tuning

As the exam draws closer, you will be bringing your preparation to its peak. Much of this will be repeating and fine-tuning areas you have already covered. Some fine-tuning activities are suggested below.

Paragraph sorting

- Go through your condensed revision notes.
- If you haven't already divided your revision topics into key themes, make a quick list of these for each topic.
- Consider whether these themes form paragraphs in their own right, or would group together into one paragraph. This may vary depending on the exact wording of each question.
- Be clear which material is the most significant, and which details either must be included or could be omitted: this can save you time in the exam.
- Consider which general paragraphs you are likely to use for different kinds of exam question on each topic.

Quick reminder list

- Identify a keyword to aid recall of each topic or paragraph.
- Produce these as a list.
- Learn the list of keywords by visualising them, repeating them aloud, and writing them out.

- Put the words to a song or story to help you remember them.

Make a single-word mnemonic

- Take the first letter of each keyword.
- Organise the letters in the order that makes them easiest to remember – either a real or a nonsense word will do, as long as you can remember what the letters stand for.

Example: 'RESPECT'

R Religious
E Economic
S Social
P Political
E Environmental
C Cultural
T Technological

Refresh your interest

If you find you are getting bored, browse through articles or books on the subject that you haven't used before. You may pick up new and interesting details, or just consider the subject from a different perspective. Reading the material with renewed interest can help you recall the overall subject.

The week before the exam: Sleep

Sleep and brain work

It is important to get enough sleep, not just from a health perspective, but to enable you to maintain high levels of attention and focus when revising and, especially, during the exam. It is possible to do well in the exam if you miss sleep, but your performance is likely to be impaired.

Manage sleep deficits

If we sleep less than we need to, which for most people is around 7 hours a night, we build up a sleep deficit. One good night's sleep doesn't cancel out this deficit so it is important to create chances to get good sleep.

In the weeks prior to the exam, build up your sleep. This will put less pressure on you to get a good night's sleep during the exam period, and will increase your chance of relaxing into sleep at night during the exam period.

Establish the right sleep pattern

Aim to establish, early on, the sleep pattern that you will need to follow during the exam period. A change of sleep pattern can disrupt the quality of your sleep and your effectiveness during the exam. If you tend to work nights and sleep during the day, consider a change in your shift pattern several weeks before the exam.

The week before the exam: Feed the brain

Common-sense eating

Basic common-sense eating patterns before and during the exam period can assist performance. Unless you have a medical condition that affects what you eat and drink, this means eating:

✔ **Proteins:** meat, fish, soya products, Quorn, nuts, cheese, mixes of pulses, grains and seeds.

✔ **Fats:** needed in order for you to process proteins and protect your gall bladder. 'Good' fats include olive oil, seeds, fish oils, other oils high in polyunsaturates. Unhealthy fats include saturated fats such as those in dairy products, some margarines and palm oil.

✔ **Carbohydrates:** slow-releasing carbohydrates such as pasta and rice prevent you feeling hungry and therefore snacking.

✔ **Fruit and vegetables:** for a range of minerals, vitamins and trace elements that maintain your health and mental functioning. Eat a varied selection.

Performance enhancement

✔ **Water**

Drink about 2 litres of plain water a day. If you drink sugary drinks, tea or coffee, then you may need to drink even more water.

Sipping water throughout the day helps electromagnetic activity in the brain. If you are relatively dehydrated, your body sends water to maintain core functions, such as keeping your heart and lungs going and digesting your food. This reduces water to parts of the brain needed to write essays or solve problems effectively.

✔ **Omega oils**

Some people who have been deficient in omega oils perform better after a course of omega oils taken for several weeks (see p. 117). These can be bought as capsules, or are available in oily fish like mackerel and in flax oils.

Foods to avoid

✘ More than 3–4 cups of coffee a day as this can affect your capacity to sleep and relax. However, see p. 117 for research on energy drinks.

✘ Sugary products, as they can lead to rapid rises and drops in energy.

✘ Food dyes, especially red and yellow, as these can make it harder for some people to focus their attention.

✘ Alcohol and drugs, as these impair mental functioning and your ability to monitor how well you are doing.

The day before the exam

There is 'a best way' for you to manage the day before the exams: this is not the same for each person. Students are very individual in their approaches to exams, to last-minute revision, and in how much stress or excitement they feel, and how they manage such stress.

Some people prefer to relax on the day before an exam. This helps them to rest, sleep better and manage anxiety. Other people find it less stressful if they feel they are using time effectively, and prefer to do final revision. You may find you can only learn certain kinds of information the day before the exam. Whatever your approach, there are some steps you can take to give yourself maximum advantage in the exam.

Plan the day in advance

Consider the best way for you to spend the day before each exam so as to remain calm and focused. Don't be pressurised into doing what others want or suggest. As far as you can, keep the day clear of all other work and activity.

'Recharge your batteries'

Make sure that you build in at least one or two changes of scene for the day before the exam, even if this is just a walk to the library. It is important that you give the brain some 'down time'. An hour or two in activity you find pleasurable will refresh your thinking and attitude.

Use the activities you have prepared to help you get in 'the zone' (Chapters 3, 4 and 11), and relaxation techniques (Chapter 10).

Practical preparations

- [ ] Select your clothes for the exam.
- [ ] Buy a bottle of water, if you are allowed to take one into the exam.
- [ ] Ensure you have necessary food supplies for breakfast and other meals.
- [ ] Pack your pens, pencils, clock, etc. Check regulations on pencil cases: are you allowed to take these into the exam room?
- [ ] If relevant, check that childcare arrangements and back-up plans are still in place.

Check details

- [ ] Use your planning checklists (p. 270).
- [ ] Check carefully the times, length, and locations of exams.
- [ ] Decide how much time you will need to get to the exam room, allowing for traffic.
- [ ] Reread the directions on past exam papers: make sure you understand these.
- [ ] Plan out the times you are likely to start each new question tomorrow.

The day of the exam

Basic considerations

- Use your checklists (see p. 271) to make doubly sure you don't forget anything.
- Leave plenty of time to get to the exam.
- Check you have maps or directions if needed.
- Make sure you have your watch or clock.
- Eat breakfast slowly – and enjoy it.
- Avoid sugars, as these can lead to a drop in sugar levels during the exam. If you have a sweet tooth, taking glucose tablets in the exam will help maintain your energy.
- Remember to take your pens, water and any equipment you need.
- Focus on positive thinking, such as how much you know for this paper, and what is good in your life, so that demotivating thoughts can't gain a foothold. Let negative thoughts float away.

At the exam venue

- Consider whether you would benefit more from talking to others or spending time on your own.
- Breathe out slowly and deeply, or use breathing exercises to calm yourself if you are familiar with these (see Chapter 10).
- Make sure you leave ALL revision notes, written material, and any other forbidden items outside of the exam room.

At your desk

- Organise your space.
- Check you can see the time easily.
- Read the instructions on the front of the paper very carefully – don't assume they are the same as last year.

Use exam time effectively

Approach

- Remain calm – speed doesn't mean panic.
- Aim to work quickly and efficiently: be businesslike about the exam.
- Advance practice can help you to develop faster working strategies.

Advance time planning

- Plan out, before the exam, how you will allocate your time. Once in the exam room, jot down the times you will start each question, and stick to this.
- Plan to leave time to read, consider and select questions.
- Identify the best questions for you – that will save time in the exam.

Planning answers

- Keep essay plans brief.
- Jot down main points only.
- Jot down any mnemonics or pieces of information that you think you might forget, as they occur to you – cross them out as you use them.
- Don't worry about neatness, unless your plan is being marked.
- Start writing as quickly as you can, even if your plans are not complete.
- If you can plan mentally, write down only what you find helpful.

Focus on key points

- Bear in mind that marks are usually allocated for covering a number of essential items in a brief, succinct way – aim to include as many of these as you can in the minimum words.
- Avoid becoming side-tracked by less important points, however interesting they may seem.
- Your personal style will shine through, but if you have a flowery or wordy style, aim to write in a more straightforward manner so you can cover the material required.

Avoid false time economies

- Make sure you organise your answers, with short but clear introductions and conclusions, and a well-structured argument.
- Don't 'save time' by just writing down 'everything you know', when marks are given for critical analysis, argument, evaluation and selection.

Selecting exam questions

Choosing your questions

- Check how many questions you need to answer for each section.
- Read each question slowly and carefully, considering what is being asked.
- Check whether there are further questions on the back of the paper: people often forget to do this in an exam.
- Mark all questions that seem possible and reread them, checking carefully how many parts there are to each question and whether you can answer all of these.
- Check very carefully the exact wording of each question (see, for example, pp. 89–90).
- You may find it helpful to scribble down quick notes of relevant material you know you could include for each answer. If you have mnemonics for certain topics, you may find it reassuring to note these down as they come to mind, using the exam paper, spare paper or the back of your exam book if there is one.

Is your favourite topic there?

If your preferred topics are there, this can build your confidence straight away. However, check very carefully that the questions really are ones that you can answer.

Favourite topics aren't there?

If your preferred topic doesn't seem to be on the exam paper, check whether it is hidden within a different question. For example, are there genuine opportunities to use material from that topic as examples within another question?

Can't answer any questions?

This isn't likely if you have revised a sensible number of topics. If you can't answer the whole of each question, then look for questions where you can give a reasonable answer to one or more sub-sections of the main question.

If the questions seem really difficult, choose subjects that you know most about and don't rush your answers. Jot down a list of possible material to include: you may remember more than you expected or know more than you realised.

Not sure which questions to answer?

Jot down a very quick outline plan to several questions. Often, even before you finish doing this, you will find you have made your mind up. If you still have several possibilities at the point where you need to start writing, just choose one and get going on it.

Answering exam questions (1)

Answer the question

- Plan your answers in brief, making sure your plan covers all aspects of the question. One quick way of doing this is to write headings with key words, references and examples beneath this. You can then add to these if you remember other points during the exam, and cross points off as you write about them.
- Keep an eye on the clock, so that you don't spend too long on any one point.
- Check, as you write, that you are still answering the question that is written on the question paper, not one that you have reworded in your own mind.
- Keep checking back to the exam paper and to your outline plan to make sure you are keeping to the set question and including all the key information you had planned.

Apply the conventions

In higher education, you are required to follow academic conventions such as:

- using an acceptable essay structure;
- providing evidence and/or examples to support the main points of your answers;
- writing in a formal style – rather than in a chatty or journalistic way;
- providing a reasoned argument, based on

critical analysis of theories and evidence, rather than just describing, narrating or listing what other people have written;
- demonstrating that you are aware of the main theories and research findings for the subject.

'Write to impress'

Students are often encouraged to 'Write an answer that draws the examiner's attention.' This is sound advice. However, this usually means that you should draw the examiner's attention in specific and accepted ways, such as:

- taking an unusual but well-reasoned approach to the question, with evidence to support your answer;
- demonstrating an unusually deep understanding of the subject;
- writing with a good style, using good grammar, syntax, spelling and punctuation;
- referring to research or a text that is unusually advanced for the level of the subject, though relevant to the subject.

Answering exam questions (2)

Think 'different'

Consider that the examiner may be reading dozens or hundreds of answers to the same question during this exam, and may have done this many times before, either as an examiner or for coursework. Most answers are likely to refer to the same basic set of theories, research and examples, and use similar arguments. This is to be expected and the examiner will not be expecting anything unusual.

However, before the exam, it is worth reading around the subject, using reputable sources such as recent journal articles or monographs on the subject. Consider how you might be able to draw upon this more unusual material in the exam. If you have several such items prepared, one or more opportunities may arise in the exam to make use of them. On the other hand, if the opportunity to use the material doesn't arise naturally, avoid distorting your exam answers merely to include unusual material.

Think 'clarity'

The examiner will want to identify quickly and easily where your answer meets the marking criteria and will appreciate a clear writing style and well-organised answer. Where answers are jumbled, with odd tangents, poor introductions and conclusions, poor paragraphing, an unclear line of argument, poor proofreading, words missing, and other features that make the answer hard to understand, the examiner will find it harder to award marks.

● Clarify your thoughts: work out what message you really want to communicate. Be clear what your position is – that is, what is your main point of view or key argument? State this in your introduction and refer back to it in your conclusion.

● Think through the best order for the points you want to make, so as to develop a reasoned argument.

● Use an opening sentence for each paragraph to link it to the one that came before, showing how this paragraph contributes further to your position.

● Select details and examples that support your position. Use a light touch with these rather than obscuring your argument in too much detail. Be clear why the evidence that supports alternative points of view is less convincing than that which supports your position.

● In your conclusion, draw together your reasoning to show how it supports your main argument.

Answering exam questions (3)

Avoid gimmicks

Don't try to draw the examiner's attention by use of gimmicks, such as:

- jokes,
- long or irrelevant quotations,
- sweeping statements about life and the universe,
- lists of questions,
- underlining points to make them stand out,
- pictures, unless the subject requires these,
- using different colours, unless required,
- laying out answers in bizarre ways on the page.

Avoid 'waffle' and repetition

Avoid saying the same thing in a long-winded and repetitious way, simply to cover the exam paper with writing. You won't get marks for making the same point twice but in different words.

Compare these two examples, noting how much relevant material is covered in a few lines.

Example 1: focused response

The shape of a volcano is also affected by the chemical composition of the lava. Relative differences in the amount of aluminium and magnesium affect viscosity, which, in turn, influences how the lava will be expelled and how far it will flow. For example, Hawaiian volcanoes are flat because of the high aluminium content of the lava, which enables it to flow in thin flat layers.

Example 2: 'waffle'

Volcanoes are amongst the most extraordinary of the natural forces on the planet. Much of the earth's topology is determined by the long-lasting effects of volcanic activity over many hundreds of millions of years. However, not all volcanoes are the same. Indeed, we can notice many different shapes. What is it that leads to such differences between volcanoes? Why are some flatter and others more conical in shape? Many answers have been put forward over the years.

Check your answers

- Plan your exam so that you have time either at the end of each question, or at the end of the exam, to check over each answer.
- Read through your answers, ensuring that they are clear and make sense.
- If material has been added later, make sure this follows the required conventions (e.g. numbered at the end of the paper, or as footnotes).
- Rewrite any words that may be illegible.

Frequently asked questions

Should I plan out essays at the beginning of the exam, or before each question?

The best approach for you will be learnt through experience, so if you haven't done exams recently, try this out by doing 'mock' exams. However, it is worth spending a few minutes at the start of the exam jotting down the key information for each essay answer. This will help with:

- checking whether you really can answer the questions you have selected;
- identifying whether you need to spend more time on some answers;
- stimulating your memory;
- feeling you are more in control of the exam.

As you work through the exam, if ideas and information come to mind about a question you have yet to do, jot it down so that you don't have to worry about remembering it. When you come to start your later questions, your mind will already have given them some thought, which will help you.

Should I write my best answer first?

This depends on whether:

- your answers improve as you warm up, or deteriorate as you become more tired;

- you feel more confident by getting your best question finished or by getting the most difficult question out of the way first;
- you are good at keeping to time. If you are poor at exam time-keeping, don't leave your best question until last.

Should I spend more time on my best question?

This is not usually a good idea. Aim to spend around the same amount of time on each question that earns the same marks. If you have to do 3 essays in 3 hours, for example, then spend roughly 50 minutes on each. Your first goal is to ensure you pass each question. It is easier to amass the basic marks needed to gain a pass answer for all questions than it is to gain sufficient marks from one or two outstanding answers.

Should I take breaks?

Some people find it refreshes them to have planned breaks of a few minutes between each question. For others, planning out a new question serves as sufficient break. Avoid breaks if stopping makes you feel anxious about wasting time.

Frequently asked questions (*continued*)

What if I go blank in the exam?

This isn't uncommon, so don't worry about being the only person it happens to – and it can be managed so that it isn't a disaster.

- Aim to remain calm. Panic makes it harder to think clearly so managing anxiety is your first concern.
- Move on to another point rather than trying to force the memory. The material you are trying to remember may come back later.
- If you are really stuck, write rough notes on a piece of paper, following possible connections, and the ideas may start to flow again.
- If no ideas come, keep the pen moving, if only to doodle or free-associate.
- Reread the question and jot down keywords. Some of these may stimulate ideas that take you to the material you need.
- If you can't remember an occasional point or reference, keep this lapse of memory in perspective. It may not be ideal not to include that information, but it isn't worth worrying about. The details you are looking for may come back to you before the end of the exam.
- You may be tired. Take a few minutes' break to calm yourself. If you have practised breathing or calming exercises, use these now.

What if I finish early?

It is normally best to stay in the exam room. Exam questions are designed to match the time available. Use the time to review your answers and check whether you have missed any important points. Using the strategies listed under 'What if I go blank' can help bring material to mind. Once you leave the exam room, you lose the opportunity to add further material.

I don't seem to use as much paper as other people

As long as you meet the requirements for each question, there is no virtue in covering paper for the sake of it.

After the exam

I've failed!

It isn't unusual for people to feel they have failed. The probability is that you will have passed. If not, you may be able to resit exams or take an alternative option or module. If you are certain you will need to do resits, then you have time to review your material. Check whether any resit workshops are offered at your university.

Check the dates for exam resits and make sure that you are available to attend these. Put some time aside to consider how you could improve your performance if you do have to resit the exam (see p. 211).

Why didn't I . . . ?

It is very common to realise, once out of the exam, all the things you could have done better. It is rare for anyone to write a perfect answer or to cover everything they might have liked to include. Don't brood, but note anything you could do differently next time.

I was ill

You should report illness at the time, before the exam if you miss it, or during the exam if you need to leave it early.

If you have a known disability or condition, you should notify staff when you arrive at the university so arrangements can be made to meet your needs (p. 255, Appendix 1). A medical certificate or equivalent is normally required if alternative arrangements are to be agreed.

It's over so why don't I feel happy?

In the lead-up to the exam, we can assume that everything will seem wonderful once the exam is over and that we will be glad to do things we had to put aside during the preparation period. However, the end of exams can bring different responses. It may feel:

- **euphoric** It feels wonderful that the exams, and revision, are over.
- **liberating** We can focus on other things.
- **anti-climactic** There seems to be nothing else so important to do any more.
- **depressing** The excitement has nowhere to go.
- **powerless** It can be hard waiting for the results.

Allow yourself time to recover from exams in your own way. You may be delighted to go out celebrating, but you may prefer some quiet time to return to life as normal.

The lessons learnt

What could I do better?

At some point not long after the exam, it is worth jotting down some notes about the lessons learnt from this set of exams. Store these so that you can find them easily when you have your next set of exams.

Reflection on exam performance	
How well did you manage your time and your revision in the lead-up to the exam?	What did you wish you had done differently once you were in the exam room?
	What have you learnt about the methods you need to use to remember information under exam conditions?
In retrospect, would you have benefited from revising more with other students, or less?	
	How did you feel after the exam? Is this what you expected? What environment do you need after an exam?

Closing comments

Summary **Key points**

★ Don't cut down on sleep before exams – it helps you absorb and recall material.

★ Before the exam, create strong mental images and checklists; follow these once in the exam.

★ Read the exam paper at least twice and in detail.

★ Keep focused on the set question; avoid both waffle and writing down all you know.

★ Manage your time so you complete all questions.

★ Write well-organised, structured answers.

★ Demonstrate clear thinking and critical analysis.

★ Proofread for errors and check for fluency.

If you have worked through some or all of this and the previous chapters you will now be in a good position to approach your exams with confidence.

Chapter 3 introduced the concept of working towards your potential personal best, or peak, performance, along with a 5-point plan to help you achieve this. If you have followed this plan, you should be feeling rested and well nourished, knowledgeable and well practised in answering exam questions, mentally alert but relaxed.

It is impossible to control for all the variables of an exam, but it is possible to know that you have taken charge of those aspects that are within your control. The 5-point plan, and chapters within the book, have identified the steps you need to take in order to succeed. These emphasised the importance of taking charge of your attitude, finding a point of calm, and searching out the enjoyment and interest within the challenge that exams present.

The ideal state for entering the exam is one where you feel you have done what is needed to achieve your own personal goals, that you have a good understanding of what to expect and of what you are able to deliver, and a well-founded confidence that you are now in a position to achieve your goals.

If you approach your exams in this way, it is all the more likely that you will enter the 'exam zone' described in Chapter 3, where everything seems to 'flow' just as it should. Your preparation can enable you not only to succeed in your exams, but even to value and enjoy your exam experience.

Chapter 13

Multiple choice question exams (MCQs)

Learning outcomes

This chapter supports you in:

- understanding what examiners are looking for in multiple choice exams
- knowing how multiple choice questions are structured
- interpreting different kinds of multiple choice questions
- revising for MCQ exams
- devising strategies for managing MCQ exams
- getting into the zone for MCQ exams

Introduction

You may be asked to answer multiple choice questions (MCQs) as a separate exam paper or as one set of questions within a paper that combines short and longer answers.

MCQ formats allow examiners to ask a wide variety of questions. You may be presented with documents or diagrams to analyse, or numerical calculations, clinical case studies, photographs, maps, DVDs, audio material or other stimulus materials. You may be asked one or more questions that require you to interpret the material correctly.

Much of the material covered in earlier chapters applies to multiple choice exams, too. As for any exam, you will achieve higher marks if you adopt a constructive attitude, plan well, organise your material, and undertake plenty of practice.

However, there are ways that MCQs differ from other kinds of exams. They create their own kinds of challenge, calling for different kinds of strategies. This chapter offers strategies to help you better understand and manage MCQ exams.

Multiple choice question exams (MCQs)

About MCQs

Typically, multiple choice exams use closed questions and a choice of 4–6 answers.

- You can't be 'nearly' correct; choices are either right or not.
- Unlike most other types of exam, it is possible to gain 100% for MCQ exams. This can help your motivation when preparing for them.

Multiple choice: An easy option?

Students sometimes under-revise for MCQ exams, assuming that they will be easy or that they will be able to guess the answers. However, note that:

- Questions are often set in such a way that they are easy to answer only if you have revised all the material; this can make them more demanding than essay-based exams.
- Many of the options may be partially correct – and so, therefore, not the right choice. You need to know your subject well in order to recognise correct options.
- Penalties may be imposed for wrong answers; depending on the size of these, guessing may be a risky strategy.

Memory and MCQs

MCQ exams test the ability to recognise the answer rather than testing memory for facts. However, if you are able to complete answers from memory, you can work with less stress,

greater confidence and speed, leaving more time for questions that need more thought.

Hey! Haven't you two got an exam tomorrow?

Yeah! It's OK. It's only multiple choice.

Reflection — MCQ exams

What is your own approach to MCQ exams?

Does this work well enough?

If not, what do you think could be better about your strategy?

What are examiners looking for?

Breadth of knowledge

MCQs can be spread across all or most of your course material, so examiners can test that you have engaged with all aspects of your programme of study.

Understanding

MCQs can be designed to check your understanding rather than memory. You could be presented with a text, documents or case study and asked questions that test your ability to interpret the information based on background knowledge or techniques covered on your programme.

Problem-solving skills

MCQs can test your ability to apply theoretical knowledge to a practical problem or to use mathematical formulae.

Thinking skills

MCQ questions are often designed to be challenging, encouraging you to think carefully and reason logically.

Attention to detail

Items that appear to be 'trick' questions are often worded that way in order to test your attention to detail.

Professional competence

MCQs can test a broad range of work-related situations, drawing on case studies and practical issues you could encounter in the workplace. The questions can be designed and clustered to check your ability to apply the right approach to the context.

Activity

Check your programme handbook and past papers to identify why MCQ exams are used on your programme and what these test.

The structure of multiple choice questions

<table>
<tr><td colspan="3">The structure of MCQ exam questions
Multiple choice questions consist of the following four aspects:</td></tr>
<tr><td>1. Instructions (check whether you will lose marks for incorrect guesses)</td><td></td><td>For each question, tick the box next to the answer you think is correct. (One mark will be awarded for each correct answer and deducted for each incorrect answer.)</td></tr>
<tr><td>2. A question</td><td></td><td>Which of the following is not a capital city?</td></tr>
<tr><td>3. A choice of responses</td><td></td><td>☐ London   ☐ Glasgow</td></tr>
<tr><td>4. A method of indicating your choice (s)</td><td></td><td>☐ Tunis   ☐ Wellington</td></tr>
</table>

Find the 'stem'

Each question generally contains words that can be turned into a 'stem statement'. If you can isolate the stem, this will make it easier to identify what you are being asked.

For the question:
Which of the following is not a capital city?

the stem would be:
… is not a capital city

Apply the stem to each of the choices, so you can test out which sounds correct. For example:

London … is not a capital city

Tunis … is not a capital city

Glasgow … is not a capital city

Wellington … is not a capital city

This can help you to recognise correct and incorrect answers. If you are still not certain of the answer, at least you may be able to eliminate some incorrect answers, reducing the options.

Revising for MCQ exams

Consider which of the strategies below you can use more effectively for your own revision; tick the boxes to remind yourself which items to come back to and use.

Focus your reading to sharpen recall

MCQs test knowledge in precise ways. Rather than simply rereading or browsing through your course notes, use more focused approaches.

☐ Read notes and texts in shorter bursts.

☐ Pause frequently to check whether the material would lend itself to a MCQ.

☐ Jot down onto cards any MCQs that occur to you, using one card for each Q and A.

Plan to manage 'breadth'

For MCQs you generally need to revise everything. To help manage this:

☐ Keep up with coursework week by week.

☐ Review it regularly, even if only to browse your notes to refresh what you covered.

☐ Summarise factual information onto cards. Carry these around, checking them frequently.

Test understanding

☐ Check that you understand the significance of theories, concepts, theorems, case studies and research studies relevant to your subject.

☐ Consider how you would test someone else's understanding of these through multiple choice, or 'true/false' question-and-answers.

☐ Consider what kind of case studies or stimulus materials (maps, photos, etc.) could be used as the basis of questions in the exam. Test yourself using these.

Design your own MCQs

Designing your own MCQs in the style of past papers helps you to work in an active way with course material and to remember it. It also helps you to enter the mind-set of the examiners and to anticipate the kinds of questions that you can prepare for.

☐ Identify how each part of your programme could be tested through MCQs.

☐ Check how past questions were designed and worded.

☐ Devise sets of closed questions and answers. Write these on cards as above. Use as 'flashcards'.

☐ Revise with other students; test each other.

☐ Think about what you would consider as 'trick' questions – and prepare for these.

MCQ: 'The answer is in the question'

Read carefully and clarify the task

In MCQ exams, the most common reason for losing marks is misreading the question. If there seem to be too many correct choices, it is likely that you need to read the question with more precision.

✔ Note the exact wording used.
✔ Use the stem separately for each choice (p. 216).

Rephrase questions

Rephrase complicated questions so that it is clearer what is being asked.

✔ Put them into your own words so they make sense – retain the sense of the original.
✔ Rephrase into 'true/false' choices (p. 219).

Convert negatives

'Negatives' (*not, never, neither this nor that,* etc.) are easy to overlook and more difficult to interpret.

✔ Rephrase negatives so they read as positives.

Example: **Which of the following is not a son of Queen Elizabeth II?**

(a) William (b) Charles (c) Andrew (d) Edward.

Rephrase as positive statement(s):

Which of the following *are* sons of Elizabeth II? (Charles, Andrew and Edward.) Which one(s) then remain? (William)

Qualifiers

Qualifiers are words that narrow or define your choices. Common types of qualifiers are:

● **words defining time:** never, always, during, prior to (X date);
● **superlatives:** the most, the least, the highest;
● **specific circumstances:** whenever X occurs, if X is the case …, assuming X …, unless …

An answer that appears correct at first may cease to do so once you check the qualifiers. For example, the two questions below would call for different answers from the choices (a)–(d).

Example: **Large or largest?**

Q: 'Which of the following is a large number?' **Choices:** (a) 4 (b) 12898087 (c) 6256798 (d) 7
A: Choices (b) and (c) would apply.

Q: 'Which of the following is the largest?' **Choices:** (a) 4 (b) 12898087 (c) 6256798 (d) 7
A: (b) – only one answer can be the largest.

True or false statements

Typically, *true/false* tests provide you with a statement, or series of statements, each of which you must identify as true or false.

> **Example**
> It always rains in Britain.
> ☐ True ☐ False

Check for false statements

● Where part of a potential answer is 'false', then the whole statement must be false – even if some aspects are true.
● The opposite is not true: if part of an answer is true, that doesn't necessarily apply to the rest of the statement. Continue to check each part of the statement in case any is false.

Qualifiers in true/false questions

Absolutes: Where the qualifiers are words such as 'always', 'the only', 'the best', 'never', this sets up conditions that are harder to meet. It is less likely that something always or never occurs, so the answer is more likely to be false. Check this possibility first – though don't rely on it as a rule.

Generalities: Qualifiers such as 'sometimes', 'might', 'rarely', 'in general' leave greater possibilities that something could occur. Such qualifiers tend to lead to 'true' answers. Check this possibility – though don't rely on it as a rule.

> **Rephrase MCQs as true/false options**
> If you are unsure of an answer in an MCQ exam, it may be easier to identify the answer if you convert the question into a set of true/false options.
> ● Identify the stem (see p. 216).
> ● Rephrase into 'positives' (see p. 218).
> ● Apply the stem to each choice of answer, asking yourself whether the statement is true or false.
> ● If more than one choice appears to be true and you are allowed more than one answer, then select all that you consider to be true.
> ● If more than one choice appears to be true and you are allowed only ONE answer, then select the answer that you consider to be 'most true'.

Avoid risky strategies

Be wary of advice that suggests that you can second guess the answer based on the structure or content of one or more of the choices. Examiners will be aware of strategies used by students who don't know the material, and so they may design questions in such a way as to prevent those strategies from succeeding.

Decide whether each of the following is a sound strategy

Put a tick ✔ beside those you consider to be a sound strategy:

(a) ☐ I haven't used option (D) yet so I'd better use it for one of the next few answers.

(b) ☐ I have used the third choice for several answers in a row, so it must be time for a different choice.

(c) ☐ The examiner has provided much more information in this choice than for all the other choices. It is more likely that this is the right answer or they wouldn't have bothered – I'll choose this one.

Answers
For answers, see p. 273.

(d) ☐ One of my choices is 'all of the above'. I can see that two of the three statements above are correct so it is likely that 'all of the above' is the right choice. I'll go for that.

(e) ☐ One of my choices is 'none of the above'. I know one of the choices is correct. This means that the answers can't be 'none of the above'.

(f) ☐ Examiners are more likely to set questions where the answer is a positive statement than a negative. I am not sure of the answer so I'll choose the positive statement.

Checklist: Strategies for answering questions

For each of the strategies below, tick box 1 (✔) if this is a strategy you already apply well and systematically. If not, tick box 2 if you think this is a strategy you want to apply in future.	Box 1 Do now	Box 2 Will do
1 **Read instructions** Familiarise yourself with the instructions for the exam – follow these carefully.		
2 **Note how many choices you can make** Can you select just ONE answer, or several?		
3 **Find the stem** Read each question carefully, identifying the stem (see p. 216).		
4 **Rephrase a negative stem as a positive** Negative words such as *no, not, never, none, neither this nor that*, etc. make questions more complicated. Rephrase the stem so that it reads as a positive (see p. 218).		
5 **Provide your own answer** Before looking at the choices, see if you know the answer. Then check whether that is provided as a choice.		
6 **Use the stem** Apply the stem to each of the choices, to double-check your answer and to see whether any other choices could also apply. If you don't know the answer, using the stem may help you spot the right choice.		
7 **Check for qualifiers** If you are unsure of the answer, check for qualifiers such as *all, always, the most, sometimes, when ..., if ..., whenever ..., both this and that*, etc. Make sure that the qualifier is included in your stem, and apply this to each choice. This may eliminate some choices.		
8 **True/false** Rephrasing the stem and each answer as true/false statements can help you spot correct answers or eliminate incorrect ones.		
9 **Eliminate unlikely answers** If you can't spot the correct answer, use your subject knowledge and logical reasoning to reduce your number of choices. Work out which of the remaining choices is the most likely.		
10 **Best guess?** If there is no penalty for a guess, then guess rather than leaving blank. If there is a penalty for an incorrect answer, weigh up the probability of whether your guess is right or wrong.		

MCQs: The day of the exam

Be prepared

- Allow time to arrive ahead of the exam, at the right place, with the right equipment (see p. 201).
- If you are taking your exam online at home, then eliminate all distractions, clear a quiet space and make sure you are not interrupted.

Read the instructions

- Read all initial instructions carefully.
- Check each question's instructions and wording carefully in case these vary.

Browse the whole paper

Gain a sense of:
- how many questions you need to answer – so that you can pace yourself well;
- the topics covered – so your brain can start to search for information on those topics;
- the focus of questions and the wording used – so you can think through anything unexpected;
- which questions will take you the most time, so that you can plan out your time accordingly.

Use the time effectively

- Work quickly but steadily.
- Don't rush your reading and checking of answers: this leads to mistakes.
- Stay focused. A little time lost between each of many MCQs adds up to a lot of lost time.
- Use any spare time to check carefully through the questions and your answers – you may have misread something earlier.

Apply your strategies

- Remain calm. Apply any strategies you have practised for managing stress (see pp. 163–73).
- Apply the question-answering strategies that you practised before the exam (see p. 221).
- Apply the strategies that you have planned for taking either paper-based or computer-assisted exams (see pp. 223–4).

Use your knowledge and reasoning

- Apply reasoning and logic in order to make a sensible guess if you don't immediately recognise the correct answer.
- Avoid taking risky strategies (see p. 220).

Managing paper-based MCQ exams

For each of the strategies below, consider whether you already use this strategy effectively. Indicate this with a tick (✔). If not, consider whether this is something you could do, or adapt, in future paper-based MCQ exams.

	Self-evaluation of study strategy	Already do this	Could do this in future
1	**Apply all the strategies on the strategies checklist:** page 221.		
2	**Best order** Work steadily through all the questions to which you know the answer or can work out the answer easily. This ensures that if any difficult questions take up more time than others, you won't miss out on marks for questions you could have answered later in the paper.		
3	**Keep track of completed answers** Circle lightly but clearly any questions to which you will return later. Erase each circle when you complete the answer.		
4	**Trouble-shoot** Mark any questions likely to consume your time. Decide how you will deal with them, depending on the proportion of marks they carry. If they carry few marks, leave them until last.		
5	**Plan and track your time** Once you complete the questions that were easiest, count how many questions remain. Divide your remaining time between these. Keep track of how you are using time.		
6	**Highlight key words in the questions** such as negatives (*no, not, never, un-*) and words or qualifiers that help circumscribe the issue (*ever, always, whenever, if ...*) dates, names, timescales, specific circumstances.		
7	**Devise personal strategies** Use your practice at mock papers to identify personal strategies that suit you and fit the style of the MCQ exam papers used for your programme.		

Reflection

Where do you currently lose marks for paper-based MCQs?

What strategies will you use to improve your MCQ exam practice?

Managing computer-based MCQ exams

For each of the strategies below, consider whether you already use this strategy effectively. Indicate this with a tick (✔). If not, consider whether this is something you could do, or adapt, in future computer-based MCQ exams.

	Self-evaluation of study strategy	Already do this	Could do this in future
1	**Prepare your space for online exams** Switch off phones; shut down other programmes; have paper and pens to hand.		
2	**Find out whether you can return to questions** The technology may, or may not, allow you to return to questions, or a screen of questions, that you have missed out.		
3	**If you can move backwards and forwards through the questions** adapt strategies as for paper-based MCQs such as covering up answers with your hand. Keep track of unanswered questions using paper and pen if there isn't an online facility to do this.		
4	**Familiarise yourself with the on-screen workspace** Identify any tools available to you as part of the test, such as a timer, or buttons and links that enable you to move between different kinds of information. You may be able to adapt the workspace to a different colour or adapt the font if that is helpful.		
5	**Use the reading time** For online tests, you may be given a set amount of time to read the instructions and/or questions before you are allowed to start answering them. Focus your attention so that you use all the time available. Don't rush the reading time – read at a reasonable pace, checking carefully what is required.		
6	**Devise personal strategies** Use your practice at mock papers to identify strategies that will suit you and which fit the style of the MCQ exam papers used for your programme.		

Reflection

Where do you currently lose marks for computer-based MCQs?

What strategies will you use to address this?

Multiple choice practice questions

For each of the following questions, identify which answer or answers are correct. One mark will be awarded for each correct answer and half a mark deducted for each incorrect answer. For answers, see Appendix 7 (p. 273).

Q1: Which of the following are not capital cities?

(a) Rome   (b) Rio de Janeiro
(c) Lagos   (d) New York
(e) Santiago   (f) Sydney

Q2: Which of the following is not a type of blood vessel?

(a) Artery   (b) Vein
(c) Vesicle   (d) Capillary

Q3: Which of the following statements is not true of William Shakespeare?

(a) Married to Anne Hathaway
(b) Wrote *Dr Faustus*
(c) Founder of the National Theatre
(d) Wrote *Troilus and Cressida*
(e) Born in Stratford-upon-Avon
(f) Had 8 children

Q4: What is the square root of 16?

(a) 8   (b) 4
(c) 256   (d) 32

Q5: Which of the following is not a possible explanation of sudden loss of consciousness?

(a) Drop in blood pressure   (b) Head injury
(c) Blood loss   (d) Boredom

Q6 Which of the following is the longest river in Africa?

(a) Amazon   (b) Nile
(c) Zambezi   (d) Limpopo

Q7: Which of the following is the least likely to be true of depression?

(a) Low mood
(b) Sleep difficulties
(c) Loss of appetite
(d) Panic attacks
(e) Lack of interest in activities

Q8: What is the square of 9?

(a) 81   (b) 3
(c) 18   (d) 99

Multiple choice practice questions (continued)

Q9: Latha has 2 brothers. The younger brother is half her age; the older brother is half as old again as the younger brother. If Latha is aged 24, which of the following statements is true?

(a) The younger brother is aged 10
(b) The older brother is aged 18
(c) The younger brother is aged 12
(d) The older brother is aged 30

Q10: Mark got 100% of his multiple choice exam questions correct. Which 2 of the following are most likely to be true of Mark?

(a) Mark guessed the answers to all the questions
(b) Mark had an effective strategy for multiple choice exams
(c) Mark is naturally intelligent
(d) Mark knows the exam subject matter well
(e) Mark revised 3 key topics for the exam

Q11: Which of the following are not types of pasta?

(a) Tagliatelle   (b) Fusilli
(c) Al dente   (d) Penne
(e) Mascarpone   (f) Rigatoni

Q12: At a university, 40 students take courses in both physics and maths. Half of students taking physics also take maths. A quarter of maths students also take physics. Which of the following statements are false?

(a) There are a total of 200 students taking physics and/or maths courses at the university
(b) There are 60 students who take maths but not physics
(c) There are a total of 120 students taking both maths and physics courses
(d) There are 120 students taking maths but not physics
(e) There are 80 students studying physics
(f) There are 140 students studying maths

Q13: Which 3 of the following have won the Nobel prize for peace?

(a) Mario Vargas Llosa
(b) Toni Morrison
(c) Barack Obama
(d) Liu Xiaobo
(e) Nelson Mandela

Q14: Which composer wrote 'Air on a G string'?

(a) J. S. Bach   (b) W. F. Bach
(c) C. P. E. Bach   (d) Mozart

'Getting in 'the zone' for MCQs

Which of the following would you find helpful for getting in 'the zone' for MCQs?

☐ Smart opponent

Consider the exam as an 'opponent' that you must outwit – such as at chess, boxing, etc.

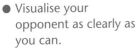

- Visualise your opponent as clearly as you can.
- How will your opponent be trying to outwit you in the types of questions set or the way they phrase the answers?
- How will you outmanoeuvre your opponent?
- Before you go into the exam room, remind yourself of the moves your opponent may make and how you are set to counter these.

☐ Hurdles

- Consider each type of question as a different hurdle.
- Develop your brain's 'muscle memory' for different kinds of question by practising each type many times.

Approach the exam as a hurdles race

- Go over your strategy for answering different kinds of question the day before the exam.

- Before you start the exam, picture yourself clearing the hurdles with ease.

☐ Specialist subject

For each exam, act as if you are on a quiz show answering questions on your specialist subject.

MASTER Student

- Write out questions and answers and rehearse these, to build your confidence in your specialism.
- Consider the most difficult questions that could be set – and prepare and practise a strategy to answer these.
- Before you enter the exam, visualise yourself in the contestant's chair answering all questions quickly and confidently.

Reflection 📖 MCQ exams

What kinds of images or scenarios help you to build the right motivation and mind-set for approaching MCQ exams?

How would you apply these to your revision?

How would you apply these on the exam day?

Closing comments

The summary below gives you an overview of how to approach MCQ exams. It is provided in the form of a checklist so that you can:

- double-check that you haven't missed anything when reading the chapter that you might now consider useful;
- consider how material in this chapter relates to that presented in earlier chapters;
- check off the items as part of your own preparation for the exam, if that would be helpful.

Key points – as a checklist

Done

☐ Be clear why MCQs are set for your programme – so you understand what examiners are looking for.

☐ Identify how strategies useful for many kinds of exam, as outlined in earlier chapters, are relevant to you when taking your MCQ exam.

☐ Use revision strategies that fit MCQ exams.

☐ Be systematic in applying a set of strategies for answering each multiple choice question.

☐ Practise finding and rephrasing the stem of multiple choice questions so that the question is as clear and easy as possible to understand and answer.

☐ Practise converting questions with confusing use of negatives into positive statements that can be eliminated.

☐ Practise converting questions into true/false statements.

☐ Consider how you will manage the MCQ exam on the day, depending on whether it is paper based or computer based.

☐ Consider how you will get yourself into the best state of mind for peak performance in the exam. See also Chapters 3, 4 and 11 on getting in 'the zone'.

Chapter 14

Managing different types of exam

This chapter supports you in preparing for:

- 'open book' and resource-based exams
- oral examinations
- oral examinations with presentations
- oral examinations with posters
- short answer tests
- technical questions

Introduction

The previous chapters have focused especially on essay-based and MCQ exams. However, it is not unusual for universities and colleges to set many different kinds of exam-based assessment. This has the advantage of allowing them to examine a broader range of knowledge and skills. If you don't shine in one kind of exam, you may find that you perform better in others.

The challenge is that, although much of what is true in preparing for one kind of exam will apply to others, some aspects will be distinct. For each type of exam, you need to consider:

- What is specific about this kind of exam?
- How appropriate to this kind of exam are the strategies and approaches that I used for other types of exam?
- How should I adapt my current strategies, or develop completely new ones, for this kind of exam?

This chapter looks at a few of the more common kinds of exam that you may encounter besides essay-based and MCQ exams.

Open book and resource-based exams

In open book and resource-based exams you either take materials such as books and notes into the exam, or materials are provided for you to use. Although you can spend less time memorising information, you do need to put time aside to prepare carefully for these exams.

What are examiners looking for?

Examiners want to see how well you:

- demonstrate your understanding of course material;
- apply information to problems or tasks, usually under timed conditions;
- recognise, select, summarise and critically evaluate information;
- think – and argue your point – when you don't have to rely on memory.

Reflection 📖 What kind of exam?
The nature of the exam should guide your preparation. Find out what kind of exam will be set. Use that information to guide your planning.

Types of exam

Open book exams vary. Find out whether you:

- ☐ can bring in whatever materials you choose
- ☐ can take in books but not your own notes
- ☐ are provided with books or other resources in the exam
- ☐ can use calculators or other equipment
- ☐ will be in an exam room
- ☐ will be taking the exam in class
- ☐ can take the exam at home
- ☐ take the exam under timed conditions
- ☐ will need to write essays in the exam
- ☐ will have short answer questions to write
- ☐ will have MCQs to answer
- ☐ will need to find solutions to problems
- ☐ will have a practical task to complete

Other details of your exam:

What happens in open book exams?

Open book exams are very flexible. They are used especially on programmes that lead to professional and vocational qualifications such as law, medicine, engineering, architecture and design, horticulture, and statistics.

In such professions, you would make frequent use of background materials to check for facts, formulae and precedents and apply these to live problems in the workplace. Open book exams can be better for testing the kind of skills you would need to apply in real life.

What would I do in the exam?

You might be asked to…

- plan or complete a practical project, client brief or a case study drawing on material covered on the course;
- write essays or short answers or answer MCQs;
- apply course material to a new situation presented in the exam;
- analyse relationships within data sets;
- critically evaluate material that you bring into the exam or that is provided for you.

You can't just 'copy from the book'

You won't gain marks simply for providing facts or writing out information if that is available in the exam. Because you don't have to remember as many facts, open book exams place a high premium on how well you use information. To do that well, you need a good understanding of the subject.

> *Example*: **Architecture project**
> You might be set a design project to complete over several days, bringing together your knowledge, understanding and skills in areas such as planning, space, materials, engineering, drawing and design.

> *Example*: **Legal case**
> You might be given, in the exam, the outline of a real or mock case and asked to:
> - state what is significant about the case;
> - identify previous legal judgments that provide relevant precedents;
> - present arguments for either the defence, the prosecution or both;
> - identify the likely outcome of a case, based on previous cases that you can cite.

> ### Activity
>
> Use materials such as your course handbook, website and past papers in order to find out:
>
> - the reasons that open book exams are set on your programme of study;
> - the kinds of questions set.

Preparing for open book exams (1)

The following strategies help in open book exams. For each item, use the first box to identify those you think would be helpful for you. Use the second box to select those strategies you want to improve.

Engage with your course

As you are not being tested for memory, you will be expected to show that you have engaged actively with your course as preparation for the exam.

- ☐ ☐ Attend the required taught sessions.
- ☐ ☐ Complete tasks set outside of class.
- ☐ ☐ Undertake independent reading.
- ☐ ☐ Think about the issues.
- ☐ ☐ Think through what is relevant or significant in the topics covered on the programme.

Make connections

Be prepared for exam questions or tasks that require you to bring together knowledge and skills from different sessions or parts of the course.

- ☐ ☐ Think how different topics might be linked.
- ☐ ☐ Consider how topics covered in one part of the course might be relevant to other parts.
- ☐ ☐ Be aware of how theoretical and practical aspects of your course are relevant to each other.
- ☐ ☐ Consider the range of technical or specialist skills you have learnt on the course – and

how these might be tested together within a single larger task relevant to your subject.

Know your materials

- ☐ ☐ Familiarise yourself with the materials you plan to take into the exam – so you know precisely which ones are best for what kinds of topic or task.
- ☐ ☐ Check the Contents and Index pages of books you can take into the exam, to see how helpful these are for quickly finding the information you need.
- ☐ ☐ Write your own index or checklist for the materials you can take into the exam room – to help you find information in these at speed.

Select the right printed materials

- ☐ ☐ Consider what tasks or questions you could be set – and the material you would use for each.
- ☐ ☐ Identify the *one* best source for each kind of question or problem that you might be set. Using one good source may save you time.
- ☐ ☐ If you are bringing in more than one source on a topic, know exactly what additional purpose you would use each one for.

Preparing for open book exams (2)

Organise your material

- [ ] Insert your own bookmarks in books.
- [ ] Write clear headers on the bookmarks to indicate what the page is useful for.
- [ ] Write the page number on the bookmark.
- [ ] Highlight key information on the page.
- [ ] Colour code text to find different kinds of information quickly.
- [ ] Draw together onto separate cards or sheets information of the same kind – such as quotations, exemplars, formulae, names and dates.

Using your own notes in exams

- [ ] Sift out any unnecessary pages.
- [ ] Condense long notes down to key points.
- [ ] Use headers to each page and section.
- [ ] Use colour tabs to signpost useful material.
- [ ] Write an index of your own notes.

Practise

As for any exam, practise as much as you can in working through the kinds of questions or tasks that you are likely to be set in the exam.

- [ ] Practise finding facts at speed. Time yourself. If it takes longer than you think, consider how to further organise your materials for easy use.
- [ ] Practise completing tasks in the time allowed. Note where the time goes.
- [ ] Consider where you can save yourself time in using the materials you take in.
- [ ] Evaluate how well you answer the question – what else do you need to know or do better?

Other relevant sections

Working with your notes – see pp. 146–9
Mock exams – see pp. 155–7
Planning exam time – see pp. 203, 208–9
Managing stress (Chapter 10)
Getting into 'the zone', Chapters 3, 4, 11, 13

Resource-based exams

For some open book exams, you do not take your own materials into the exam room. Rather, you answer questions on texts or other resources that you see for the first time in the exam. Usually, these are the same or similar to materials that you would have used already on your course.

Example: **Extracts from historical texts**

You may be asked:

- what kinds of documents they are and how you can tell;
- the probable date, author(s) and purpose;
- why these are significant historically;
- to translate documents, for example from medieval English into modern English;
- to demonstrate that you can identify most relevant information in the documents.

Example: **Literature exams using poems or extracts from texts**

You may be set questions that show you:

- can recognise the author and/or genre;
- can analyse texts using approaches appropriate to literary criticism;
- are aware of what is significant within the text(s) or about the text(s);
- can relate the text to other texts, drawing out relevant comparisons and points of contrast.

Example: **Sciences and social sciences**

You may be asked to use materials provided in order to critique the methodology of a piece of research, showing you are aware of concepts covered during the course.

Preparing for resource-based exams

Make sure you are familiar with the source materials relevant to your area of study, whether texts, documents, statutes, slides, artefacts.

- Make a list of features that experts in your subject look for when using such resources.
- Make your own glossary of technical terms that you will be expected to use when referring to, or describing, the resources.
- Practise analysing resources, identifying their most significant features; consider how you would describe these to a non-expert.
- Practise identifying key features 'at a glance', to build your exam speed.
- Consider which resources, if any, you are likely to be set for seen or unseen exams, and practise working with these.

Tips for open book and resource-based exams

✔ Prepare well: don't assume this is an easy option just because you have materials with you.

✔ Consider resources you take into the exam as 'back-up' only, for checking occasional details. Revise your material as you would for other exams.

✔ Be up to date with your coursework and reading.

✔ Consider how different aspects of your course link up – exam questions may require you to integrate material drawn from across your course.

✔ Condense and organise your materials so you can find what you need quickly and easily.

✔ Make glossaries, checklists and summary sheets that help you to locate materials at speed.

✔ Practise working with materials at speed, so you become used to moving quickly between items.

✔ Take just what you need into the exam – and no more. Too many resources slow you down.

✔ Most marks are awarded for your own words. Avoid copying material from books and resources.

✔ If you quote from a source, keep it short. Provide a reference in the style required on your course.

✔ In the exam, scan the materials to see which are most useful to the questions. Mark sections with stickers and tabs so that you can find them easily.

✔ Manage your time: share it between questions according to the marks they carry.

Reflection

● What tips and strategies are priorities for you to develop for your next open book or resource-based exam?

● How will you go about putting these into practice?

Oral exams: Why are they set?

1 To test spoken language ☺

To see how well you express yourself verbally:

- in a foreign language;
- or in particular kinds of spoken tasks relevant to the programme or professional area – such as with clients, patients, customers, children or research participants.

2 To test depth of knowledge ☺

To check your understanding of course material:

- by following up on your answers more flexibly than is possible in written exams;
- by giving you a chance to talk about a topic or project you have worked on in depth;
- by checking individuals' understanding of work undertaken in groups.

3 To provide interest and challenge ☺

In this case, examiners are looking less at how well you speak, and more at the content. They use oral exams to:

- vary the methods of assessment;
- develop skills in thinking, speaking, presenting under pressure, and also interpersonal skills – all useful for employment and for life generally;
- prepare you for presenting papers at academic and professional conferences.

What kind of oral exam is it?

If you have been set an oral exam, find out which of the following will be tested.

☐ Language proficiency
☐ Spoken skills for specific audiences
☐ Subject knowledge
☐ Presentation skills
☐ Other skills

Check if there will be:

☐ A solo presentation
☐ A group presentation
☐ A poster-based presentation
☐ Practical work with oral answers

Other:

Reflection Oral exams

- How do you feel about taking oral exams? Are these an area of strength?

- If not, what prevents you from performing well in oral exams?

Oral exams: Getting in 'the zone'

You can't force entry into 'the zone', but you can help that state of mind to emerge.

Know your material

Prepare for oral exams as you would for other exams. Cover all your coursework, condensing it down, checking for understanding, and organising it to help recall.

Write, record, listen, respond

- Write out sets of questions and answers.
- Read these aloud and record them.
- Make a podcast of the recording so you can listen to the Q and A in spare moments.
- Listen back to your answers several times, repeating them aloud, so that they start to become automatic responses.

Practise aloud

- Ask and answer questions aloud so that you can 'hear' the Q and A in your head; this will help with recall in the exam.
- Practise in front of the mirror and/or to friends.
- Record yourself answering questions aloud: note whether you stick to the point.
- Practise Q and A sessions with other students.

The night before

- Prepare a final checklist of things to do next day, with a timeline for doing for these.
- Browse quickly through material that you have already rehearsed, so as to aid recall.
- Summon up visual images of you travelling to the exam room, greeting the examiner with a warm smile, waiting calmly for questions you have practised, and providing answers in an even, fluent way that does you credit.
- Set your mind to welcome the exam with a 'constructive edge' – such as a challenge you want to face or as a means of excelling.
- Leave time to have a reasonable night's sleep, so that the brain absorbs your vision of the exam and organised material ready for the exam.

On the day of exam

- Keep your mind occupied so there is no room to dwell on nerves.
- Check over your material.
- Work methodically through your checklist of 'things to do'.
- If you have time, undertake some light physical exercise so as to release pent-up energy.
- Focus on practical details.
- Remind yourself of your 'constructive edge' before you go into the exam.

Oral exams: In the exam

Interpersonal skills

- Arrive in good time, dressed smartly and, if required, with your slides, handouts, posters or other material ready.
- Switch off phones and any equipment not needed for the exam.
- Present yourself professionally, using good eye contact and body language. Greet the examiners politely and give your name.
- Smile and be pleasant but avoid distracting the examiners with questions and small talk.
- Examiners assume students may be anxious. You will look more professional if you just focus on the questions and avoid apologising for nerves, forgetfulness or personal problems.
- Thank the examiner politely at the end. Avoid asking for feedback on the spot.

Answering questions

- Listen to the question carefully and without interrupting – work out what is being asked.
- Pause before answering; check you have understood the question.
- Ask the examiner to repeat the question if you need to check you understood it.
- If a brief answer is required, keep your answer short. However, it is rarely sufficient to answer with just 'yes' or 'no'.

- For open-ended questions requiring longer answers, organise your thoughts briefly before answering.
- If you don't know the answer, see if you can work out logically what it might be.
- Focus on each question in turn – avoid worrying about any you couldn't answer.
- When you have finished answering the question, stop speaking. Avoid rambling on or repeating what you have already said.

'Dynamic' question sessions

- Questions are sometimes asked dynamically – that is, follow-up questions are based on your previous answers in order to check the extent of your knowledge.
- Examiners may continue a set of questions on one issue until you run out of answers, before then proceeding to the next set of questions.
- Focus on your answers and avoid analysing how well you are doing: it may be hard to tell.

 © Stella Cottrell (2006, 2012) *The Exam Skills Handbook*, Palgrave Macmillan

Oral exams with presentations

Deciding on your topic or angle

If you are given the opportunity to choose your topic or angle, take time to select one that will enable you to perform at your best.

- Browse articles, titles of book chapters, podcasts and websites for inspiration.
- Choose a topic that engages you – your enthusiasm will help to engage the audience.
- Find an angle that will be new to the audience in some respect – even if only the examples or presentation of data.
- Consider how you will focus the topic, if necessary, to fit the time available.
- Narrow the focus sufficiently to give you time to include interesting examples and to do justice to any data or difficult material.

Researching your subject

- Read up on the subject – so that your presentation comes across as well informed.
- Pick out only the most essential material – you can include far less information in a presentation than in an essay.
- Condense material to a minimum.
- Identify examples and data that illustrate your argument and that add interest.

Shaping your presentation

If you are preparing your presentation electronically, select a design template for your slides.

- Decide the main message that you wish to communicate.
- Use your second slide to sum up your main message in around 10–30 words.
- Devise a title that encompasses your message; write this in as the first, 'title', slide.

Preparing the presentation

- Use your third slide to introduce the talk, indicating why the topic is important, what the issues are, and what you are going to cover.
- Decide how many natural sections there are to your material; create a slide for each.
- Select material that will enable you to speak for 2–3 minutes for each slide at a speed slightly slower than everyday speech.
- If you use tables or charts, keep these simple so their key messages are self-evident and so they do not take you long to explain.
- Rehearse your presentation, timing how long it takes. Ask a friend to listen so you can check that your pace of delivery is appropriate.
- It is likely that you will find it a challenge to cover all the material you would like.

Good presentations

The allocation of marks for presentations varies, depending on which skills are being assessed. What is 'good' for an examined presentation will depend on why a presentation was set as a piece of assessment. However, some useful guidelines are outlined below.

Presenting the material

As with good exam essays (p. 87), presentations should:

- have a clear focus: decide the key messages you want to get across;
- be constructed as an argument;
- present your argument from the beginning, to help the audience to follow the direction of your talk;
- be selective, identifying the most salient points;
- be well organised, so that each point follows logically from the one before and stands out clearly;
- consider and evaluate different points of view rather than just presenting your own position.

Holding the audience's attention

The importance of holding the audience's attention will vary depending on the marking criteria: check how marks will be allocated and for what. When they are listening to others,

people usually like clear 'signposting' to help them identify where each point fits into an overall argument. These are good ways to hold the audience's attention:

- Consider that 'less is more': avoid overloading the audience with complex data or information. Select only the most important items, so the audience can absorb them.
- Break your presentation into a few, short, numbered sections, so the audience can monitor where you have got to in the presentation.
- Time your presentation carefully so you don't need to rush. Avoid talking faster in order to fit in more information.
- Talk slightly more slowly than normal speech.
- Provide a visual aid to each person, such as a chart or a short handout of the key points, or else use a projector.

Using slides

- Avoid small print – use large font sizes.
- Include no more than 4–7 lines per slide.
- Use no more than one slide per 2 minutes of speech.
- Ensure that each slide's heading sums up the topic of that slide clearly.
- Don't simply read out what is on your slides, as this will bore the audience – paraphrase them.

Oral exams with poster presentations

Use of poster presentations is widespread as a means of assessment in higher education and for presenting information at conferences and in the workplace. Making a poster can be a relatively enjoyable way of preparing for, and starting off, an oral exam.

You can be individual in your approach and use images, colour, shape, graphics, data, humour and captions in interesting ways.

Problem elaboration

Making a poster can be fun. Nonetheless, it also requires skill in balancing several different kinds of task simultaneously. You need to:

- Work out what is really being examined – and ensure you meet the marking criteria.
- Focus on a single key issue; select an angle that lends itself to poster presentation.
- Be clear of the overall messages that you want to communicate.
- Jot down a list of areas that you will cover.
- Consider how best to divide up information into a few large sections for the poster.
- Balance the quality of your information with making a visually attractive poster and clarity in getting your message across.
- You may need to give more thought to the medium – that is, what you will use in order to construct your poster – than would be the case for other assignments.

Posters need to be balanced

Clear messages	*v.* Over-simplification
Using design and visuals	*v.* Visuals over-dominating
Being informative	*v.* Information overload
Using academic content and theory	*v.* Being over-abstract and dull
Appealing to an audience	*v.* Playing too much to the audience

Strategy for poster-based exams

Get organised

Designing and making a poster can be quick and easy if you hit upon a simple and effective idea from the outset. However, students often find that making posters can eat into their time, if they let it. Typically, you need to put time aside to:

- Think of a good idea and research it.
- Reduce down and organise the material.
- Design and make the poster.
- Practise your presentation.
- Practise answering potential questions.

Manage your time

- Calculate how much time you are willing to spend on the poster.
- Write a list of all the things to be done.
- Allocate an amount of time to each.
- Build in time to practise.
- Stick to your time limits – it is all too easy to keep finding ways of fine-tuning a poster.

Be aware of your audience

Consider your target audience at all times:

- What content is appropriate to them?
- What will they want to know the most?
- How much information can they absorb, realistically, in the time?
- How can you hook your audience through interesting ways of presenting the information?

Select material wisely

- Stay 'on message' – cut out anything irrelevant.
- Be concise. Avoid losing your headline messages with too much detail.
- Avoid simply reproducing a whole report in the form of a poster.
- Use graphics and visuals to reinforce your verbal messages.

Consider the visual aspects

The design, layout and images are part of the message. Visually, the poster should:

- be appropriate for the audience;
- convey the message at a glance;
- ensure the heading or title stands out clearly;
- present material clearly – and lead the eye logically from one section to another;
- look professional, neat and attractive.
- make your audience keen to look at it, read it and think about it.

Reflection

Consider how you might you produce your poster electronically. You could make use of software such as PowerPoint, Microsoft Publisher, Keynote (Mac) or Impress (open source).

Poster layout

Here are four examples of how a poster might be laid out:

The title stands out – because of font size, location, colour.

The overall design and flow of information can be grasped immediately by the eye.

Numbering, arrows or connecting lines lead the eye logically around the poster.

Related information is grouped and linked visually by use of shape, colour and sub-headings.

Empty spaces give the viewer's eye room to rest, and bring out the design and message.

Dense information is kept to a minimum and contained visually so as not to overwhelm viewers.

Charts, tables and images convey information visually.

References are provided.

Headings, images, colour and other design features are applied consistently, to provide coherence to the overall poster.

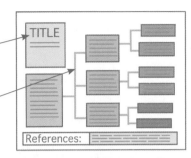

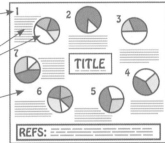

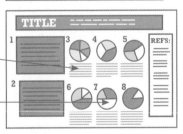

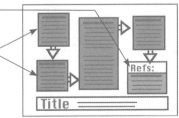

'At a glance' evaluation of posters

For posters, although the content is important, so too is overall visual impact; otherwise the audience may not even read excellent material. Smith et al. (2004) found that scientists' responses to posters presented at neurology conferences indicated that 'An unattractive poster with high scientific merit risked being overlooked on first impression.' For the following posters, consider how well the design features draw in the viewer and communicate key messages 'at a glance'. See Appendix 7 for feedback.

1

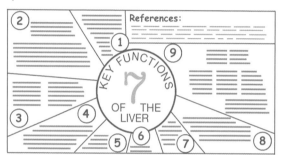

3

2

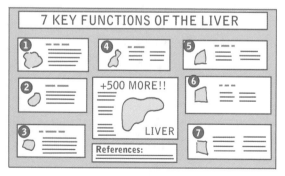

4

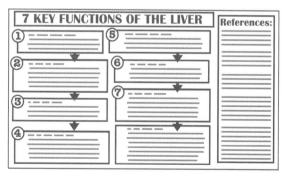

Poster presentation checklist

	Item to check	Action to take to improve	Done ✔
1	The poster focuses on one central issue or question?		
2	The title conveys what the poster is about?		
3	The title is written large and stands out visually on the poster?		
4	The overall message of the poster stands out 'at a glance'?		
5	The poster is divided into clear segments or sections?		
6	There is a clear heading to each section?		
7	The sections are organised logically on the poster?		
8	Colour or graphics are used well to indicate different sections?		
9	All writing on the poster is in a legible font size and style?		
10	Text in each section is brief, concise and to the point?		
11	There are plenty of empty spaces, for the eye to rest?		
12	Images and/or quotations are used to add interest/humour?		
13	All images and text are appropriate to this audience?		
14	The eye is led logically around the poster using graphics or arrows?		
15	Graphics are used to summarise key information where relevant?		

Poster presentation checklist (*continued*)

	Item to check	Action to take to improve	Done ✔
16	Graphics are easy for other people to understand at a glance?		
17	There is not too much information for the target audience to digest?		
18	The content is all appropriate and relevant to this audience?		
19	The content is all relevant to the assignment and title?		
20	Information has been edited down to essentials?		
21	Sources of information are referenced?		
22	Overall, the poster looks professional, neat and attractive?		
23	Design features are applied consistently, providing coherence?		
24	I have made a handout of background information (if relevant)?		
25	I know how I am going to talk about my poster for my presentation?		
26	I have rehearsed what I will say to present my poster?		
27	I have jotted down a list of questions I might be asked?		
28	I have rehearsed answers to the questions I might be asked?		
29			
30			

Presenting the poster

Using posters in oral presentations

✔ Prepare the room so that you can display your poster to best effect. Welcome and greet your audience.

✔ Structure your presentation as you would for any talk, with a brief introduction, a main body and a conclusion.

✔ Make sure the poster is visible to all of your audience.

✔ Start by stating the title, drawing attention to it on the poster.

✔ Give your reasons for choosing this topic, indicating why this is significant in general and for the audience.

✔ State the key message you want to convey.

✔ Introduce your talk, outlining the main sections, indicating why they are included, and where they are on the poster.

✔ Continue to refer to the poster throughout your presentation.

✔ Work through the different sections of your poster, always making sure the audience knows to which section you are referring.

✔ Provide background information as handouts if this is useful and permitted.

✔ Invite comments and questions from your audience. Where possible, refer to a specific part of the poster when making your answer.

✔ To conclude, sum up what you have said, referring back to your key message or the title.

After your presentation

✔ Maintain a professional approach.

✔ If relevant to the context, remain near your poster so as to answer questions.

✔ Smile and welcome those interested in looking at your poster.

✔ Let readers have time and space to take in the key features of the poster.

✔ Don't crowd readers – but ask if they have any questions you could help with.

Short answer tests

What is a short answer test?

- Short answer tests require answers shorter than those typical of essay-based papers.
- Questions can range from multiple choice questions through to explanations and descriptions of several paragraphs.
- Answers are usually factually based – unlike essays, which tend to be more analytical and creative.
- Typically, you are asked to define a term, perform a calculation, identify a source or quotation, and/or give examples.
- You may be asked, additionally, to comment on why the quotations or data provided are significant or to explain the issues.

What are examiners looking for?

Examiners use short answer tests to:

- Check the *depth* of your knowledge base in the subject: the questions tend to require detailed factual knowledge of a particular area.
- Check the *breadth* of your knowledge: several short answer questions mean that more areas of the course can be tested.

Types of short answer questions

Typically, short answer questions are used when the answer required involves one or more of the following:

- listable items, such as the key functions of organs of the body, or key features of a piece of equipment;
- the main aspects of a particular theory, and reasons for its significance;
- stating where a quote comes from in a set text, and providing reasons for its significance;
- providing a diagram or details of a simple experiment, which wouldn't be sufficient to form the basis of a long answer question;
- details of specific procedures, such as how to manipulate a limb, produce a chemical under certain conditions, or deal with a specific mathematical problem;
- the main similarities or differences between two groups that are often contrasted.

Preparing for short answer tests

Revise well

Unlike essay-based questions, where you can usually choose to revise a smaller number of topics and leave out some without too great a risk, for short answer tests you need to know all of your course material well.

Organise your material

- Summarise programme material into questions followed by lists of key points.
- Make a checklist of key definitions, specialist terms, controversial issues, and significant dates and facts – revise the list systematically.
- Write out and learn succinct and precise definitions of key terms.
- Look for ways of further condensing your summary answers.

Identify good examples

- Identify examples that best illustrate key concepts and themes, so that you can draw upon these at speed in the exam.
- Consider how you would word examples in a concise way in the exam – sometimes the name, date and a few key words that indicate a piece of research or theory will suffice.
- If relevant to the subject, write out short quotes (of a few words only) to exemplify points that you might wish to make.

Use 'flashcards'

- Write out your questions and answers onto index cards; use one card per question.
- Make a numbered list of the key issues for each question.
- Write out formulae, definitions or quotations.
- Write a few succinct sentences that sum up – and join up – the information.
- Carry cards around with you so that you can refer to them in a 'little and often' approach.
- Make good use of spare moments to revise.

What time is the number 82 bus due?

After the French Revolution

Preparing for short answer tests (*continued*)

Count out the points

There is usually a specific, and countable, number of points to make for short answers. For example, if you are asked to outline the role of a certain vitamin in the body, or list the properties of halogens or describe the working of an engine, there will be a set number of commonly acknowledged or prescribed items that the examiner looks for. When revising:

● Identify what such countable items would be for each question you are revising.
● Write that number next to the question, as a reminder of how many items you need to recall.
● Set out your revision material so that each item is visibly distinct.
● Number each item.
● Enumerate each item, either in your head or aloud, as you revise it.

Practise

● Invent as many realistic questions as you can, based on those that have appeared in past papers. This will increase your chances of having practised the questions that will be set for your exam.
● Answer these under test conditions.
● If you do not know the answer, use logic and common sense to identify potential answers or sensible guesses.
● Note whether you are tempted to include irrelevant material or to write in an excessively wordy way just so you have something down on the page.
● Check your answers against your notes to see how well you remembered the information.
● Develop memory-joggers to help recall under exam conditions. See pages 126–33.

Edit your practice answers

● Read through your answers, checking each point against the question set.
● Put a line through any material that is irrelevant to that question. Be strict with yourself.
● Note how much material you crossed out – this represents time that could have been spent on another question.
● Note whether the relevant material is written as succinctly as it might be. If not, practise rewriting your answers so that they are brief, condensed and to the point.

Taking the exam: short answer tests

Use time strategically

Check the marks given for each answer. Divide your time according to the marks carried by each.

- Work quickly: short answers are to the point and don't usually require planning out.
- If the paper includes other kinds of questions such as essays, leave sufficient time to answer those.

Identify exactly what is being asked

Note how many parts there are to the question. Work systematically through each part, crossing it off as you complete it, so that unanswered sections remain visible.

- Note the process words such as *analyse*, *define*, *explain*. Follow directions exactly, doing what is asked and no more.
- Note the key terms: which specific areas of the topic are included in the question?
- Remain focused on what is asked: avoid adding unnecessary material.

Be concise – and avoid 'waffle'

If you can convey the required information in one paragraph, there is no need to use five.

Avoid padding answers with irrelevant material just to make it look as though you know more about the subject. This could lose you marks – and wastes time that you could have allocated to another question.

Structure your answers

If you are expected to write short answers of more than a few short sentences, then structure these as you would an essay, using:

- an introductory sentence to define the terms or issue;
- a sentence or paragraph on each point;
- a concluding sentence.

Make each point stand out

- Ensure that you cover all your 'countable items' for each question (p. 250).
- State each point so that it stands out distinctly. If necessary, start a different sentence for each, rather than combining two or more points within a single sentence. This makes it more likely that the examiner will identify each point and allocate marks accordingly.
- Read your answer to check that good points are not lost in complex or over-condensed sentences.

Answering technical questions

What are technical questions?

Technical questions require you to apply set procedures or mathematical formulae to resolve given problems. You are required to demonstrate that you can recognise the kind of problem being outlined, and select the appropriate method for resolving it. Accurate working and attention to sequence and to detail are also essential.

Unlike essay-based answers, there is little opportunity for personalised approaches: there is usually a set, or correct, answer. The advantage of this is that, if you know your material well, you can have a clearer idea of how well you have performed before receiving your marks from the examiners.

Revising for technical subjects

- Make sure you are aware of each specific step in calculations or procedures, and in applying formulae, and that you can reproduce these exactly from memory. There is little room for improvisation for technical questions.
- Devise mnemonics for remembering the various stages in sequences.
- Practise answering past questions as well as questions you invent for yourself, so that you are used to producing technical answers at speed.

Identify what is being asked

- Read carefully through the information you have been given, analysing it to identify the problem that needs to be resolved. From this information, you will need to decide the solution you are going to apply.
- It is important to give sufficient time to elaborating the question accurately, as this will help you to identify the right solution. Don't rush this stage.
- Think calmly and logically through the conventions and formulae you have used in class, and consider which of these are likely to apply.
- Consider which combination of procedures might lead to a solution.
- Pay attention to the details, such as the units of measurement required (grams, kilograms, ounces, seconds, volts) and make sure these are clearly identified in your own answer and in all diagrams.
- If you are required to include diagrams, use sharp pencils and proper measuring tools. Make sure the diagrams are easy to follow, clearly labelled, and legible.

Organise your answer

- Write out accurately the data that you have been given, under the heading 'Given'.
- Write out what it is you have to find, under the heading 'Find', along with a brief analysis of the data. Demonstrate that you understand what the problem is.
- Identify your approach: identify which formulae you are going to apply, and write these out, to show the examiner you know the theory. This will also help you to focus on the answer.

Elaborate the solution

- Write 'Solution'.
- Use the data you have been given to apply the formulae.
- Write down each stage of your worked answer as you go, building upon each line.
- If you come to a halt, think through the procedures you have worked on in the past, and decide which of these might apply at this point.
- As you go along, identify the procedures you are using, such as 'differentiate', so the examiner knows what you are trying to do at each stage.
- Continue until the problem is resolved.

What if I can't resolve the problem?

- Make sure you have provided clear evidence of the method you are using and your working out, as these may gain you marks even if the final answer isn't correct.
- Identify on your paper that you are aware the problem doesn't resolve.
- If you have run out of the time you allocated for this question, then leave it and go on to the next question.
- If you have time, check your working out: is the mistake a simple mathematical error on your part?
- Check back over the initial data: did you miss a clue in the information you were given?
- Reconsider the nature of the problem: did you misinterpret the nature of the problem? Identifying this correctly will help identify the correct solution.

Closing comments

Summary Key points

★ Consider carefully why the examiners have chosen that type of exam – what does it help them to find out about your knowledge or skills?

★ Think through how you will prepare for the exam so that the required knowledge and skills shine through. Avoid reverting to strategies that worked for previous exams if these are not strictly relevant to the exam you are taking.

★ Make good use of the information available to you: usually, your tutors will provide details within your programme material to guide you on what will be examined, when, how and why.

★ Practise for each type of exam. The way that you will need to select and apply information will vary for each type of exam, calling upon distinct skills.

★ Organise your revision and exam preparation so that you build your confidence, competence and expertise. For each type of exam that you are set, consider what you, personally, need to do in order to increase the likelihood of getting into 'the zone'.

Each type of exam calls for a different set of revision and exam strategies. It does pay to think through, and in some detail, exactly what is being examined in each kind of exam and how you can best prepare for each.

However, there isn't a need to reinvent the wheel for every kind of exam. The skills that you may have developed and applied in one kind of exam are likely to be applicable, at least in part, to other types of exams that you might be set. Similarly, many of the approaches to exams and revision and strategies for achieving peak performance covered in earlier chapters will apply to most kinds of exam.

Appendix 1

Alternative exam arrangements for students with disabilities and/or dyslexia

What are my rights?

Universities in Britain are required to make adjustments to assessment arrangements for students with disabilities including dyslexia, dysgraphia and dyspraxia, where such adjustments are 'reasonable' and do not affect academic standards.

However, there can be considerable waiting times for students with disabilities to gain what they require. It is sometimes necessary to book specialist support such as BSL (British Sign Language) communicators several months in advance. It can also take time to purchase specialist equipment or furniture. The more advance notice you give the university or college, the better placed they will be to put the right support for you into place.

What kind of alternative arrangements can be made?

The adjustments are usually made on an individual basis, depending on the severity of the disability or condition and the type of examination. Some examples of typical arrangements are:

- If you use British Sign Language or Sign Supported English as your main language, and find you work slowly or with difficulty in English, you can request to take your exams using an interpreter.
- Students who use Braille can request Braille technology.
- For some medical conditions and disabilities, students have been given rest times within exams.
- Students with motor difficulties or some forms of dyspraxia and dysgraphia have dictated answers to a scribe who writes down exactly what they say.
- Where students have a genuine reason why their answers may take longer to produce, they may be given additional time to complete

them.

- Students who have severe attentional difficulties may be offered a different room in which to take their exam.
- Students with some disabilities who use voice-activated computers have taken their exams in a separate room and dictated their responses to a computer.
- If you can, request adapted furniture and technology, to meet specific needs.

Who should I tell – and when?

You should inform the university as soon as you can, preferably long before the first term starts. It can take a long time to organise assessments to identify what is needed for your particular disability on the course of study you are pursuing.

It also takes time to set up the alternative arrangements and to organise the funding for these. The earlier you tell the university, the more likely it is that they can locate specialist staff and resources to meet your needs.

Most colleges and universities in Britain have an Equality Service, Disability Officer or Coordinator, who will be able to advise you on the next step to take. Otherwise, contact Student Services or their equivalent. You can also talk to support staff in the student union at your college or university.

What evidence do I need of my disability?

If you had alternative arrangements made for recent exams at another educational institution, then send evidence of this to your college or university, along with any assessments made by doctors, audiologists, educational psychologists or other specialists.

If you think you have a condition that has not been diagnosed, the Disability Officer at your university or college should be able to advise you on the next step to take. As many students request such diagnoses at the beginning of the year, there can be waiting lists, so the earlier you make enquiries, the better.

Appendix 2

Might I be dyslexic?

Wouldn't I know by now?

A number of people wonder whether they might be dyslexic or have a related condition such as dyspraxia or dysgraphia.

Many students who do have dyslexia were not diagnosed at school. This may have been because their coping mechanisms were fine for dealing with schoolwork but do not work in university or work contexts. Other people may have struggled with spelling, reading, writing, and other aspects of school, but dyslexia didn't seem the most obvious reason for their difficulties at the time.

What would be the signs of dyslexia?

The characteristics of dyslexia vary from one person to another, but tend to include some or all of the following:

- Particular aspects of reading, spelling or writing tend to remain very difficult, even after attending school regularly and making a consistent effort to improve. Reading, writing and spelling may be at relatively high levels in students with dyslexia, but remain much more difficult than other aspects of study.

- Students with dyslexia can generally understand their subjects as well as other people, but find it difficult to write down what they know in a way other people can understand.

- Dyslexic errors tend to occur in distinctive patterns, rather than as occasional spelling errors or the typical errors that lots of people make. The pattern of errors will vary depending on the type of dyslexia.

- People with dyslexia tend to have a range of other difficulties associated with balance, coordination, timing, direction and sequence. They may be good at sport, but still have poor coordination under certain conditions.

- Often, people with dyslexia demonstrate a very poor sense of time, consistently missing appointments or not being able to guess how long it takes to complete tasks.

- For some people with a related condition, known as Meares–Irlen syndrome, it can be difficult to look at a page of text for long without it seeming to move, flicker, or form patterns that make it difficult for them to continue reading. There are strategies such as using tinted papers, filters or glasses which can relieve this. Alternatively, using a larger font or increasing the space between each line of text can reduce the problem.

- Sometimes, people with dyslexia can find it hard to listen to a series of directions or instructions, remember these and carry them out in the right order.

- Dyslexia often runs in families and can be genetic, or it can be associated with premature birth.

What would happen if I told someone?

If you told the Disability Officer that you thought you might be dyslexic, it is likely that some or all of the following steps would occur.

The officer, or a specialist Dyslexia Support Tutor, would:

- Ask you to come for a chat, to talk through why you think you might be dyslexic.

- Ask you a lot of questions to find out what else might be creating your difficulties.

- Arrange an initial 'screening', involving some short reading, writing and other exercises, to get a feel for your kinds of difficulties and how these might affect your study.

- If relevant, arrange for you to see a psychologist for specific tests. Some of these involve reading and writing, but others are more general tests of ability. This can take around two hours. It can seem daunting to visit a psychologist, but many people find it an interesting experience and you shouldn't worry about it.

- After the screening or assessment, the Dyslexia Support Tutor or Disability Officer will explain the results – sometimes psychologist reports can appear technical and confusing to people who are not psychologists themselves.

- If all of the above indicate dyslexia, then you will need a further assessment to identify the support you need for your programme.

- Often, there is a different explanation, such as missed schooling, stress, or a medical condition. You would then be advised on who to see for further support to help you manage these.

Appendix 3

Sources of help

General difficulties with study or student life

- Speak to your personal tutor, year tutor or course tutor, depending on arrangements at your university or college.
- Visit Student Support Services at your university or college: they will have a range of staff who can offer advice and guidance in areas such as study skills, finance, counselling, accommodation, childcare, medical support, drugs and alcohol abuse and eating disorders. These services are confidential.
- Your student union will also have advisers who can assist you themselves or refer you to other sources of help.
- Look in your student handbook – there are likely to be local sources of help listed there, and contact names for help with different issues that you may be facing.

Literacy and numeracy courses

If you need to brush up on your English or maths, there may be classes available either at the university, or through a local college. You can also do courses online through **learndirect** or through software packages.

Study skills

www.skills4study.com   Free materials on study skills and personal development planning.

Disability, dyslexia, dyspraxia, dysgraphia

Ask to speak to the Disability Officer or Dyslexia Support Tutor (or equivalent) at your university or college.

Adult Dyslexia Organisation

Provides support to adults, especially students, with dyslexia and dyspraxia.
www.futurenet.co.uk/charity/ado/adomenu.htm
Tel: 0207 924 9559

The British Dyslexia Association (BDA)

National organisation that provides assessments, support and information.
www.bdadyslexia.org.uk
Tel: 0845 251 9002

Dyslexia Scotland

www.dyslexiascotland.org.uk
Tel: 01786 446 650

Dyslexia Association of Ireland

www.dyslexia.ie
Tel: 01679 0276

Disability Alliance UK

www.disabilityalliance.org/

General

www.direct.gov.uk/disabledpeople
UK government's disability issue website.

National Institute of Adult Continuing Education (NIACE)

www.niace.org.uk

Physical and mental health

NHS Direct
www.nhsdirect.nhs.uk
Tel: 0845 46 47 (speak to a nurse for immediate medical advice by phone)

www.studenthealth.co.uk

Samaritans

www.samaritans.org
Tel: 08457 90 90 90 (UK)
Tel: 1850 60 90 90 (Republic of Ireland)
Email: jo@samaritans.org

Appendix 4

5-point plan for peak performance

1   Want it!

Aspect	Action: What I will do and when, where and with whom	Update on the action (Is this happening to plan?)
Take charge of your attitude		
Develop your self-awareness		
Maintain a balanced perspective		
Find the interest and enjoyment		

2 Live it!

Aspect	Action: What I will do and when, where and with whom	Update on the action (Is this happening to plan?)
Rest, nourishment, water, exercise		
Create the environment		
Gain support		
Make the time		
Manage stress		

3   Know it!

Aspect	Action: What I will do and when, where and with whom	Update on the action (Is this happening to plan?)
Understand exams		
Understand your subject inside out		
Select what you really need		
Apply material to specific questions		
Identify which memory strategies work for you		

4 See it!

Aspect	Action: What I will do and when, where and with whom	Update on the action (Is this happening to plan?)
Clarify what exam success means for you		
Walk your mind through the process		
Envisage your success		

5 Do it!

Aspect	Action: What I will do and when, where and with whom	Update on the action (Is this happening to plan?)
Apply revision strategies		
Learn the material in an active way		
Practise answering exam questions		
Use revision time effectively		
Use exam time effectively		

Appendix 5

Planning checklists

Planning checklist 1: Now

Action	Comments	Done
Enter all exam dates and deadlines into your diary or planner.		
Enter into your diary or planner the date when you will start your revision.		
If necessary, arrange for time off work and rearrange any appointments that clash with your exam dates.		
Arrange for alternative arrangements for disability, dyslexia, etc. (if applicable).		
Obtain up-to-date programme material, such as the syllabus, the programme outline, learning outcomes, subject benchmark information.		
Check whether other information is available such as example exam answers, copies of examiners' and external examiners' comments.		
Obtain copies of past papers (these may be available on the website or from the college library).		

Planning checklist 2: As early as you can

Action	Comments	Done
Draw up your exam timetable, identifying broad timescales for studying each subject.		
Identify whether there are people who you could work with well as part of your revision strategy.		
Make arrangements for any sessions where you will revise with other students; note these in your diary.		
Make arrangements for childcare or work shifts, once you know the exact exam dates.		
Reduce down and organise your material (see 'Structured revision sessions', Chapter 9).		
Prepare as many questions as you can (see 'Structured revision sessions', Chapter 9).		

Planning checklist 2 (*continued*)

Action	Comments	Done
Work actively with material so as to build sets of associations (see 'Memory', Chapter 8).		
Devise mnemonics for lists, formulae, names and dates (see pp. 132–3).		
Prepare yourself mentally for the exam (see 'Getting in "the zone"', Chapters 3, 4 and 11).		
Practise as many past exam questions as you can, in exam conditions (see 'Structured revision sessions', Chapter 9).		
Check the exam venue, and plan your travel arrangements and time of arrival.		
Check whether you need to wear specific clothes for the exams, such as a gown, and make sure you have these.		
Identify what helps you sleep and what keeps you awake.		
Find ways of keeping relaxed and rested, such as walking, sport, yoga, or exercise.		

Planning checklist 3: The week before exams

Action	Comments	Done
Eat nutritious food.		
Drink plenty of plain water (see pp. 117 and 200).		
Sleep well – avoid building up a sleep deficit.		
If necessary, reduce your notes down further.		
Check your ability to reproduce your mnemonics.		
Check any necessary equipment is in working order, has batteries, etc.		
Re-check the exam venue and travel arrangements.		
Prepare maps and directions if necessary. Know how long the journey will take.		
Confirm cover for work and for care arrangements.		
Make sure you have a bag you feel comfortable leaving away from your desk.		
Make sure you have a clock or watch for the exam room.		

Planning checklist 4: The day before exams

Action	Comments	Done
Eat meals with slow-releasing carbohydrates, protein, fruit or vegetables.		
Make sure you are properly hydrated: drink plenty of plain water (see pp. 117 and 200).		
Work off restless energy and anxiety through exercise, yoga, or a brisk walk.		
Use relaxation methods to manage stress; build in some time for enjoyment if this will help you relax.		
Check last-minute details and your mnemonics if you think this will help.		
Re-check that any necessary equipment is in working order, has batteries, etc. Buy pens, pencils, etc., as needed.		
Re-check the exam venue and your travel arrangements.		
Re-confirm cover for work and for care arrangements.		
Set at least one alarm clock, if your exam is in the morning.		
Sleep well – avoid revision and stressful tasks and thoughts before going to bed. Create a relaxing atmosphere.		

Planning checklist 5: The day of the exam

Action	Comments	Done
Eat light meals with slow-releasing carbohydrates, protein, fruit or vegetables. Heavy meals can make you sluggish.		
Take water with you to the exam.		
Take a clock or large-faced watch with you so you can see the time easily. Synchronise this with the exam-room clock when you arrive.		
Use relaxation methods that work for you to manage stress. Take action to maintain a sense of calm.		
Take additional jumpers or jackets in case you feel cold in the exam.		
Check last-minute details and your mnemonics if you think this will help.		
Re-check that any necessary equipment is in working order, has batteries, etc., and that you have this with you.		
Make sure you have details of the exam time, venue and directions to the exam room with you.		
Make sure you have your pens, pencils etc.		
Leave all valuables at home.		
Make sure you have a bag with you that means you can meet requirements for leaving notes, etc., away from your exam desk.		

Appendix 6

Tracking developments in an area of research

Date of publication	Name(s) associated with the research	Key findings	Significance/ impact of the findings	Other comments and details

Appendix 7

Answers to activities

Answers to 'Risky strategies'

(e) is a sound strategy as it must lead to a correct answer. All of the others are not sound because they are guessing at particular ways of thinking on the part of the examiner. Although these approaches are sometimes recommended, they are not good strategies since they could very easily lead to incorrect answers.

Answers to multiple choice practice questions (Chapter 13)

Q1: The answers are (b) Rio de Janeiro, (d) New York and (f) Sydney; these are *not* capital cities.

Q2: The answer is (c). A vesicle is not a type of blood vessel; it is a membrane-enclosed sac.

Q3: The answers are (b), (c) and (f). The correct statements are (a), (d) and (e): William Shakespeare *was* married to Anne Hathaway, he *was* born in Stratford-upon-Avon and he *did* write *Troilus and Cressida* – but remember, the question was 'Which statements are *not* true'. He did not write Dr Faustus, found the National Theatre nor have 8 children.

Q4: The answer is (b) 4. The possible answers also include the square of 16 – 256. MCQs are often structured to provide a wrong answer which will appear correct if you have not read the question carefully.

Q5: The answer is (d) Boredom. Boredom is not a possible explanation for sudden loss of consciousness.

Q6: The answer is (b) Nile. The Nile is the longest river in Africa. The Amazon is the longest river in the world but is located in South America.

Q7: The answer is (d) Panic attacks. Although some people with depression may also experience panic attacks, this is not commonly recognised as a symptom of depression.

Q8: The answer is (a) 81. As with question 4, the possible answers contain the response to a different question about the square root of 9. Examiners will set questions that require careful reading, and often similarly worded, but quite different, questions will appear close to each other on the exam paper. It is important to read each question carefully.

Q9: The correct answers are (b) and (c). If Latha is 24 and the younger brother is half her age, the younger brother must be aged 12. If the older brother is half as old again, he must be 12 + 6 = 18 years old.

Q10: The correct answers are (b) and (d). It is most likely that Mark has an effective strategy for multiple choice exams and knows the subject matter well. Although it is possible to guess every answer and get 100%, it is highly unlikely, and more likely to gain a mark of around 25%. Natural intelligence does account for some exam success but Mark would have been unlikely to achieve 100% without employing additional strategies. If Mark had only revised 3 topics he might have been very lucky and only faced questions on these topics. However, this is unlikely and multiple choice exams generally call for breadth of subject knowledge.

Q11: The answers are (c) and (e). Al dente is a phrase which means 'to the bite', which refers to the texture pasta should have when perfectly cooked. Mascarpone is a type of Italian cream cheese. Tagliatelle (flat noodles), Fusilli (twists), Penne (quills) and Rigatoni (large ridged tubes) are all types of pasta.

Q12: Statements (b), (c) and (f) are false. If 40 students study both physics and maths, then twice as many students must study physics in total = 80; four times as many students must study maths in total = 160; 40 of those students are 'double counted' as they study both subjects. Consequently, there must be 200 students in total. 120 students study maths but not physics (three-quarters of the total amount of those studying maths). 40 students study physics but not maths (half of the total amount of those studying physics).

Q13: The correct answers are (c), (d) and (e). All of the choices are Nobel prize winners. The three winners of the Nobel prize for peace are Barack Obama (2009), Liu Xiabo (2010) and Nelson Mandela (1993). Mario Vargas Llosa (2010) and Toni Morrison (1993) both won the Nobel prize for literature.

Q14: The answer is (a), J. S. Bach. Both W. F. Bach and C. P. E. Bach were sons of J. S. Bach and composers in their own right. It is common for MCQs to have a number of very similar sounding answers to test out how well you know your subject.

Answers to poster designs (Chapter 14)

Poster 1

✔ The title stands out clearly and the large central image may catch the eye and so attract the viewer's initial interest.
✔ References are included.
✔ Items are numbered, and there are empty places for the eye to rest.
✘ The weak points are that the use of a large central circle, although arresting in itself, makes it challenging to create good visual shapes within the rest of the oblong poster. The positioning of the references box adds to the visually poor layout. The overall effect is of unattractive shapes and uneven treatment of the material. There is no use of images or graphics. The numbering of 9 sections in the same style detracts from the key message that the poster focuses on 7 functions.

The positioning of the numbers is disorganised – the number appears in a different place in each box so is harder to find. Moving anti-clockwise around the circle would be confusing for many people.

Poster 2

✔ The heading and visual layout makes it easy to take in the purpose of the poster at a glance.

✔ It gives the impression straight away that the information is well organised and logical, and that the information is in digestible bites.

✔ The numbering leads the viewer's eye around a logical layout. Each separate area has its own heading and the sense of good organisation is increased as information is laid out in the same way for each of the 7 numbered boxes.

✔ There are empty places for the eye to rest.

✔ Illustrations add visual interest and may also help to explain the information.

✔ The viewer's interest is also caught by the large heading to a central area suggesting that there is more than one way of considering how many functions the liver has.

Poster 3

✔ The design leaves space for the eye to rest, which is good in principle.

✔ References are clearly included.

✔ The use of the speech bubble and blocked space as illustrations and/or diagrams provide points of interest.

✘ However, the poor layout and lack of numbering or any other signposting combine to give a sense of disorganisation. It isn't obvious where the viewer should look first nor which text is attached to which diagram. Within this disorganisation, the title isn't obvious. The use of such a large head and shoulders may attract viewers if relevant to the topic but may be just wasting space that could have been used to include interesting content that adds marks. There appears to be far too much unused space, giving the impression that the paper is not well researched.

Poster 4

✔ The title stands out clearly.

✔ The poster gives the impression of being well researched, with a strong references section.

✔ The material looks well organised.

✔ Items are numbered and there is additional signposting through the material provided by the arrows.

✔ Additional material of some kind is presented, which adds interest.

✘ The key weakness is that almost all the space has been filled with text, which can be so off-putting to readers that they do not look at the poster at all, or find it hard to keep reading. Key messages can become lost in so much information. If all the space is taken with text, then there isn't a logical reason for presenting this as a poster rather than as a written paper.

✘ Despite the strong organisational structure, the poster looks dull and uninviting. There are no images to break up the text and add visual interest. The lack of headings for each section means that it will be harder to read and absorb information, and also means that the viewer isn't drawn into the additional material provided in the final box.

References

BBC News, *Gamers get into 'the zone'*, 28 July 2002, http://news.bbc.co.uk/1/hi/technology/2154092.stm (downloaded 22 April 2006).

Carlstedt, R. A. (2004), *Critical Moments During Competition: A Mind–Body Model of Sport Performance* (Hove: Psychology Press).

Cottrell, S. M. (2011), *Critical Thinking Skills* (Basingstoke: Palgrave Macmillan).

Csikszentmihalyi, M. (1992), *Flow: The Psychology of Happiness* (London: Random House).

File, S. E., Jarrett, N., Fluck, E., Duffy, R., Casey, K. and Wiseman, H. (2001), 'Eating Soya Improves Human Memory', *Psychopharmacology*, **157**, 430–6.

Hardy, L., Jones, G. and Gould, D. (1996), *Understanding Psychological Preparation for Sport: Theory and Practice of Elite Performers* (New York: John Wiley and Sons).

Holford, P. (2002), *Optimum Nutrition for the Mind* (Grantham: Piatkus Books).

Jackson, S. and Csikszentmihalyi, M. (1999), *Flow in Sports* (Leeds: Human Kinetics Europe Ltd).

Jackson, S. and Roberts, G. (1992), 'Positive Performance States of Athletes: Toward a Conceptual Understanding of Peak Performance', *The Sports Psychologist*, **6**, 156–71.

Jokela, M. and Hanin, Y. L. (1999), 'Does the Individual Zones of Optimal Functioning Model Discriminate between Successful and Less

Successful Athletes? A Meta-analysis', *Journal of Sports Sciences*, **17**, 873–87.

Orlick, T. and Partington, J. (1988), 'Mental Links to Excellence', *The Sports Psychologist*, **2**, 105–30.

Richardson, A. J. and Montgomery, P. (2005), 'The Oxford–Durham Study: a Randomized Controlled Trial of Dietary Supplementation with Fatty Acids in Children with Developmental Coordination Disorder', *Paediatrics*, **115**, 1360–6.

Sharma, V. M., Sridharan, K., Pichan, G. and Panwar, M. R. (1986), 'Influence of Heat-Stress Induced Dehydration on Mental Functions', *Ergonomics*, **29**, 791–9.

Smith, P.E.M., Fuller, G. and Dunstan, F. (2004), 'Scoring Posters at Scientific Meetings: First Impressions Count', *Journal of the Royal Society of Medicine*, **97**(7), 340–1; http://www.ncbi.nlm.nih.gov/pmc/articles/PMC1079533/ (accessed 26 May 2011).

van Overwalle, F. (1989), 'Success and Failure of Freshmen at University: a Search for Determinants', *Higher Education*, **18**, 287–308.

Warburton, D. M., Bersellini, E. and Sweeney, E. (2001), 'An Evaluation of a Caffeinated Taurine Drink on Mood, Memory and Information Processing in Healthy Volunteers without Caffeine Abstinence', *Psychopharmacology*, **158**, 322–8.

Index